Sicilian: ... e5

SPECIALIST CHESS OPENINGS
GENERAL EDITOR: R. G. WADE

# Sicilian: ... e5

## T. D. HARDING, P. R. MARKLAND

1 e4 c5 2 ♘f3 ♘c6 3 d4 cd 4 ♘×d4

4 ... e5 La Bourdonnais (Löwenthal)

4 ... ♘f6 5 ♘c3 e5 Lasker/Argentine (Pelikan)

4 ... ♘f6 5 ♘c3 d6 6 ♗e2 e5 Boleslavsky

B. T. Batsford Limited *London*

First published 1976
© T. D. Harding, P. R. Markland, 1976
ISBN 0 7134 3208 X (cased)
ISBN 0 7134 3209 8 (limp)

Printed in Great Britain by
Billing & Sons Ltd., Guildford and Worcester
for the publishers
B. T. Batsford Limited
4 Fitzhardinge Street, London W1H 0AH
Chess Digest, Inc., P.O. Box 21225, Dallas, Texas 75211

BATSFORD CHESS BOOKS
*Adviser:* R. G. Wade
*Editor:* K. J. O'Connell

# Contents

# Symbols and References

| | |
|---|---|
| + | check |
| = | balanced position |
| ⩲ | some advantage to White |
| ⩱ | some advantage to Black |
| ± | clear advantage to White |
| ∓ | clear advantage to Black |
| ±± | winning advantage to White |
| ∓∓ | winning advantage to Black |
| ! | good move |
| !! | excellent move |
| !? | interesting but risky move/ untested idea |
| ?! | dubious move |
| ? | weak move |
| ?? | blunder |
| 1–0 | Black Resigned |
| ½–½ | Draw Agreed |
| 0–1 | White Resigned |
| Ch | Championship |
| corres | correspondence game |

W or B at the side of each diagram indicates which player is to move. In the text, a number in brackets after a move refers to the diagram of that number.

The following abbreviations in the text refer to our chief sources:

| | |
|---|---|
| AHM | analysis by Harding and Markland |
| B | Boleslavsky, *Skandinavisch bis Sizilianisch* |
| CMQ | Baumbach, article in *Schach* (translation in Chessman Quarterly 5) |
| G | Gligorić and Sokolov, *The Sicilian Defence* (Book 1) |
| K | analysis by Kottnauer and Harding |
| M | Minev, article in *The Chess Player* 4 |
| P | Pachman, *Semi-Open Games* |
| R | *Chess Archives* |
| S | Suetin, in *Encyclopaedia of Chess Openings* B |
| U | Uhlmann, in *Encyclopaedia of Chess Openings* B |
| V | analysis by Povah |

The other chief sources for recent master games were: *The Chess Player* 1–9, *Informator* 1–19, *Shakhmatny Bulletin* (to No. 1 1976).

# Preface

This book deals with three ultra-sharp lines of the Sicilian Defence which involve an early ... e5 thrust by Black. These all arise from the opening moves 1 e4 c5 2 ♘f3 ♘c6 3 d4 cd 4 ♘×d4 and comprise:

the La Bourdonnais (Löwenthal) Variation (4 ... e5),

the Lasker or Argentine (Pelikan) Variation (4 ... ♘f6 5 ♘c3 e5), and

the famous Boleslavsky Variation (4 ... ♘f6 5 ♘c3 d6 6 ♗e2 e5) together with lines analogous to the Boleslavsky that arise after other sixth moves by White.

Readers of our earlier volume (The Sicilian Richter-Rauzer) will notice that this book is in the algebraic notation—a change, dictated by the publishers, which we welcome. Algebraic is clearer and more concise than descriptive, and can be learned by anyone in a few minutes. Figurines are used instead of letters for the pieces to make the book accessible to a world-wide readership.

We should like to acknowledge extensive help with our treatment of the 4 ... e5 variation from two sources: Cenek Kottnauer, I.M., and the 1975 English Southern Counties' Champion, Nigel Povah. Their main contributions are clearly marked in the text. We have Neil Coles to thank for providing historical material, including Sultan Khan's games. Other people, too numerous to mention, helped in various ways.

The Boleslavsky has been so much accepted that players with White have been avoiding it for years. Perhaps it is time for a fresh look!? On the other ... e5 lines we have set out to challenge a lot of piously-held dogmas about the Sicilian and believe we have made as strong a case as possible for the viability of the m. We hope that you will be encouraged to try some of our recommendations, and we shall be interested to hear from readers who have played interesting games or have new ideas in these variations.

T.D.H., P.R.M.
*March 1976*

# Introduction

The Sicilian lines in which Black plays ... e5 early on are some of the most exciting variations of the whole defence. They also have the advantage for the practical player that, compared with the Dragon or Najdorf, they are not so well-known. Through ignorance of theory and the shock of being forced into unfamiliar territory, many Whites may meet, for example, the 5 ... e5 variation with an inferior plan (or no plan at all) and rapidly concede the initiative. So why is an early ... e5 not played more often?

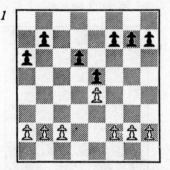

Diagram 1 may help to explain why 'respectable' positional players have tended to shun these lines. The diagram shows a typical pawn structure that arises from the ... e5 variations; Black's pawn thrust has established outposts at d4 and f4, but has left him with a 'hole' at d5 and a backward d-pawn. There are slight differences between the variations (in the La Bourdonnais the pawn is at d7 not d6; in the Boleslavsky, the a-pawn may be at a7 or a5), but it is above all the hole at d5 which makes the ... e5 variations controversial. This introduction traces the historical development of these lines up to the 1970s, showing how it is that the move ... e5 may often gain more than it concedes.

In the early decades of the 19th Century, few if any players understood the dangers of having a 'hole' in one's position – i.e. a square that cannot be defended by one's own pawns. So, even when given the opportunity of inflicting a hole upon the opponent, they often missed the chance, as in the line 1 e4 c5 2 ♘f3 ♘c6 3 d4 cd 4 ♘ × d4 e5 when 5 ♘ × c6, improving rather than disimproving Black's pawn structure, was the first move to be tried. We illustrate this with the game that originated the La Bourdonnais variation, with notes based on those in Neishtadt's book *Shakhmaty do Steinitza* ('Chess before Steinitz'). MacDonnell–La Bourdonnais, match 1835: 1 e4 c5 2 ♘f3 ♘c6 3 d4 cd 4 ♘ × d4 e5 5 ♘ × c6? bc 6 ♗c4 ♘f6 7 ♗g5 ♗e7 8 ♕e2 d5 (See page 32 for comments on the opening.) 9 ♗ × f6!? ♗ × f6 10 ♗b3 00 11 00 a5! 12 ed cd 13 ♖d1 d4 14 c4 ♕b6 15 ♗c2 ♗b7 16 ♘d2 ♖ae8 (16 ... ♕ × b2 17 ♕d3 g6 18 ♖ab1 e4!=) 17 ♘e4 ♗d8 18 c5 ♕c6 19 f3 ♗e7 20 ♖ac1 f5! 21 ♕c4+ ♔h8 22 ♗a4 ♕h6 23 ♗ × e8 fe 24 c6 ef 25 ♖c2 ♕e3+ 26 ♔h1 ♗c8 27 ♗d7 f2 28 ♖f1 d3 29 ♖c3 ♗ × d7 30 cd e4 31 ♕c8 ♗d8 (perhaps clearer 31 ... ♖d8! 32 ♖cc1 d2 33 ♖cd1 ♕e1 34 ♕c3 e3 35 ♖d × e1 de=♕ 36 ♖ × e1 ♗b4!) 32 ♕c4 (32 ♖3c1 d2 33 ♖cd1 ♕f4! – Romanovsky) 32 ... ♕e1 33 ♖c1 d2 34 ♕c5 ♖g8 35 ♖d1 e3 36 ♕c3 ♕ × d1 37 ♖ × d1 e2(2) 0–1

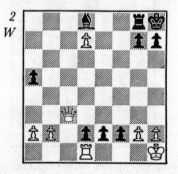

2
W

Some writers, perhaps unaware of La Bourdonnais' priority, still attribute the 4 ... e5 variation to Löwenthal, a master of the next generation, on account of the following undistinguished game. As Löwenthal did not add anything to the theory of the line (unlike Staunton: see chapter 3) the crediting of the line to the Hungarian emigré is singularly unhistorical.

Morphy–Löwenthal, 6th match game, London 1858: 1 e4 c5 2 ♘f3 ♘c6 3 d4 cd 4 ♘ × d4 e5 5 ♘ × c6? bc 6 ♗c4 ♘f6 7 00 d5?! 8 ed cd 9 ♗b5+ ♗d7 10 ♗ × d7+ ♕ × d7 11 ♖e1 ♗d6 12 ♘c3 e4 13 ♗g5 ♘g4 14 ♕ × d5 ♗ × h2+ 15 ♔h1 ♕ × d5 16 ♘ × d5 00? (16 ... ♗d6)

17 f3 ef 18 gf ♘e5 19 ♖e3 f6 20 ♔×h2 Tad8 21 ♖×e5 fg 22 ♔g3 h6 23 c4 ♖f7 24 ♖ae1 ♔f8 25 c5 g6 26 c6 ♖c8 27 c7 ♖×c7 28 ♖e8+ ♔g7 29 ♘×c7 1–0.

Later developments in the La Bourdonnais variation were slow in coming. Perhaps under the influence of Louis Paulsen, lines with ... e6 were the most popular forms of Sicilian in the 19th Century (although Paulsen is supposed to have experimented with a kind of Boleslavsky on three occasions), and the next master we find playing 2 ... ♘c6 and 4 ... e5 is Mir Sultan Khan, the Indian virtuoso, who tried it in 1930, winning all four games. However, this was early in his brief career, before he had learned more positional defences from his western contemporaries. Two of his opponents tried 5 ♘b3, one 5 ♘e2; only Apscheneek played 5 ♘b5! and it was met by 5 ... d6.

Nowadays, 4 ... e5 is almost always met by 5 ♘b5 a6 etc. (chapters 1 and 2) but that is a comparatively recent development. The Leningrad master Kuzminikh, who played the La Bourdonnais variation in several games in the 1930s and 1940s and wrote an article about it in *Shakhmaty v SSSR* (1951), had difficulties only when Aronin and Averbakh replied 5 ♘b5 – but Kuzminikh, too, was playing 5 ... d6 in reply and not 5 ... a6. It was in the 1950s and 1960s that the line 5 ... a6 6 ♘d6+ ♗×d6 7 ♕×d6 ♕f6 – called by continental writers 'Jagdspiel' ('hunt variation') because of the way the white knight and queen are chased around the board – became the most popular way of handling 4 ... e5. It is not clear who inaugurated the hunt variation; it appears in some games by Dutch players like Vlagsma, and then was enthusiastically taken up by Baumbach and other East German players around 1961–3. Since the middle sixties it has not had so many advocates at master level, but is still practised in amateur and junior chess.

One important argument against the La Bourdonnais variation is that Black's problems stem not so much from the hole at d5 as the fact that in the 'hunt variation' he has to give up the two bishops – in particular the king's bishops – leaving him with some dark square weaknesses. This is not the case with the Lasker Variation, which is one reason why we prefer it to 4 ... e5.

The line 1 e4 c5 2 ♘f3 ♘c6 3 d4 cd 4 ♘×d4 ♘f6 5 ♘c3 e5 was launched by Emanuel Lasker in the ninth game of his World Championship match with Schlechter in 1910, though the possibility was mentioned in earlier editions of Bilguer's *Handbuch*. It is noteworthy that Lasker was at this stage one game down with two games to go, so needed something sharp to give him winning chances. The game continued 6 ♘b3 ♗b4 7 ♗d3 d5! 8 ed ♘×d5 9 ♗d2 ♘×c3 10 bc(*3*)

3
B

10 ... ♗d6 11 ♕h5 ♕c7 12 00 ♗e6 13 ♗g5 h6 14 f4 ef 15 ♖ael ♔d7 16 ♗f5 ♖af8 17 ♗×f4 ♗×f4 18 ♘c5+ ♔c8 19 ♗×e6+ fe 20 ♘×e6 ♗×h2+ 21 ♕×h2 ♖×f1+ 22 ♖×f1 ♕d7 23 ♘c5 ♕e7 24 ♕h3+ ♔b8 25 ♘e6 ♔a8 26 ♘d4 ♕c7 27 ♕f5 ♖c8 28 ♕c5 ♘b8 29 ♕×c7 ♖×c7 30 ♖f3 a6 and was drawn in 65 moves.

The game Yates–Sultan Khan, British Championship, Scarborough 1930, also reached diagram 3 (by transposition) and went instead: 10 ... ♗e7 11 ♕h5 (better 11 00 00 12 f4± as in Mitrev–Ilkov, Sofia 1973) 11 ... ♗e6 12 00 ♕c7 13 ♗e3 000 14 ♘c5 ♗×c5 15 ♗×c5 ♖d5 16 ♗e3 e4 and Black won. Despite these early successes, 5 ... e5 was not often seen until after the Second World War, and as with 4 ... e5 the main problem for Black was to find a viable way of meeting 6 ♘db5. Haberditz's line 6 ... h6!? had a limited vogue in the early 1950s, but the line 7 ♘d6+ ♗×d6 8 ♕×d6 ♕e7 9 ♕×e7+ (or 9 ♘b5!) has effectively put it out of business.

At first it must have seemed that 6 ... d6 (to keep the king's bishop) was too passive, but then a group of Argentinian players realized that Black could subsequently gain a tempo by ... a6 and then attack that knight on a3 either by ... b5 (threatening a fork) or in some cases ... d5. Two names in particular are commonly linked with the renaïssance of the 5 ... e5 line – Pilnik and Pelikan. It was master Pelikan, in the 1955 Argentinian Championship, who introduced the startling pawn sacrifice 5 ... e5 6 ♘db5 d6 7 ♗g5 a6 8 ♗×f6 gf 9 ♘a3 d5!? (e.g. 10 ♘×d5 ♗×a3 11 ba ♗e6) and grandmaster Pilnik played this several times in Europe the following year, for example against Geller in the Candidates' tournament at Amsterdam.

The attraction of the Pelikan variation lies partly in the dramatic elimination of the hole at d5 by means of the pawn sacrifice. However, there are other ways for Black to approach the same issue. He can play 9 ... f5 to soften up White in the centre, reducing his hold on d5, or Black can arrange to capture a knight on d5 if White has to recapture with the e-pawn, in which case the weakness disappears. Which of these strategies Black employs depends partly on whether White plays 8 ♗ × f6 or the superior 8 ♘a3. The majority opinion among masters appears to be that the latter move gives Black some difficulties.

However, the evaluation of the Argentinian variation involves a great number of complicated variations, and recent analysis tends to show that Black's chances are much better than is generally believed. Larsen, who played the line a few times and made contributions to the theory, wrote that it was 'intended to be a surprise weapon, and if it was not 100 per cent correct I didn't mind'. Since 1973, however, the young Soviet masters Timoshenko and Sveshnikov have been playing 5 ... e5 at practically every opportunity, as it were defying their (often famous) opponents to prepare new 'refutations'. The results of this intense exposure have by and large been in favour of the Argentinian variation, and other players (notably Women's World Champion, Nona Gaprindashvili, and Junior World Champion, Valeri Chekhov) have been encouraged to take it up themselves.

However, perhaps neither 4 ... e5 nor 5 ... e5 would have achieved any post-war popularity had it not been for the example of Boleslavsky, who demonstrated in the period 1943–48 that in at least one case Black could happily play a positional game despite a hole at d5. Where one 'heresy' is seen to flourish, others may soon follow.

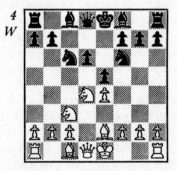

The diagram shows the position arising from 1 e4 c5 2 ♘f3 ♘c6 (or first 2 ... d6) 3 d4 cd 4 ♘ × d4 ♘f6 5 ♘c3 d6 6 ♗e2 e5, the beginning of the Boleslavsky variation. Formerly, Black would play either 6 ... g6 (the well-analysed Dragon) or Euwe's 6 ... e6 (the Scheveningen) in which Black develops quietly behind his own lines and usually has to be satisfied with a draw. Boleslavsky's insight was that, with his bishop committed to e2, White has no quick way to seize control of the d5 hole, so that Black can hit back either with his own ... d5 advance (prepared by ... ♗e6 etc.) or obtain play on the wings while the centre is kept closed. The pawn at e5 opens up possibilities of controlling d4 or f4 and allows the queen's bishop to go to e6 or g4; moreover, the attack on the ♘d4 obliges White to make an early and committing decision. Many games and analyses had by 1946 convinced most of Boleslavsky's Soviet colleagues of the validity of his idea, and so the Boleslavsky variation became an important weapon in the armoury of the Soviet team in the immediate post-war period. The Sozin and Richter–Rauzer attacks had to be further developed as methods of avoiding the Boleslavsky.

One can see the influence of the Boleslavsky on a number of Sicilian variations. The Najdorf line 1 e4 c5 2 ♘f3 d6 3 d4 cd 4 ♘×d4 ♘f6 5 ♘c3 a6 6 ♗e2 (or 6 g3) 6 ... e5 is an obvious example, and an even better one is the O'Kelly variation 1 e4 c5 2 ♘f3 a6; now 3 d4? cd 4 ♘×d4 ♘f6 5 ♘c3 e5 is a very good form of the Lasker variation, as 6 ♘b5 is impossible and the black king's bishop is free to come out to b4, with threats of ... d5 and ... ♘×e4. Was Boleslavsky himself influenced by the earlier line 1 e4 c5 2 ♘f3 d6 3 d4 cd 4 ♘×d4 ♘f6 (4 ... e5?! see p. 31) 5 f3!? e5! 6 ♗b5+ ♘bd7 7 ♘f5 d5! where Black hits back on the squares weakened by White's fifth move? Note that after 5 ♘c3 it is not good to play 5 ... e5, as 6 ♗b5+ prevents Black from transposing to the Lasker Variation, while White has not played the weakening f3, but ♘c3 which prevents the liberating ... d5.

The first Karpov–Spassky Candidates' match game of 1973 was a striking example of the influence of the Boleslavsky Variation. Since on this occasion Black played ... e5 after having already played ... e6 (i.e., with a loss of tempo), it seems that for some grandmasters at least, the soundness of the Boleslavsky is an article of faith!

Diagram 5 shows the position after 1 e4 c5 2 ♘f3 d6 3 d4 cd 4 ♘×d4 ♘f6 5 ♘c3 e6 6 ♗e2 ♗e7 7 00 00 8 f4 (8 ♗e3 e5 has been played.) 8 ... ♘c6 9 ♗e3 (a main line of the Scheveningen, where 9 ... ♗d7 is usual) 9 ... e5!? 10 ♘b3 a5. This is a mutant Boleslavsky in which Black has not played ... ♗e6 (compare Sterner–Boleslavsky on p. 94): not necessarily a bad thing. Although it was Spassky's playing 9 ... e5!? which brought it to general notice, it had already

been experimented with in some Levitina–Kozlovskaya games, one as early as 1971, and was tried again between the same players in 1974. As Hartston remarked in the *British Chess Magazine* (8/1974), 'it is no coincidence that Bondarevsky is both Spassky's second and Kozlovskaya's husband'.

From diagram 5, the Karpov–Spassky game continued 11 a4 (11 a3 a4 12 ♘c1 may be best.) 11 ... ♘b4 12 ♗f3 ♗e6 13 ♔h1 ♕c7 14 ♖f2 ♖fd8 15 ♖d2 ♗c4! 16 ♘b5 ♗×b5 17 ab a4 18 ♘c1 d5! 19 fe (19 c3 de) 19 ... ♘×e4 20 c3 (20 ♖e2 a3!) 20 ... ♘×d2 21 ♗×d2 ♕×e5 22 cb ♕×b4 23 ♘d3 ♕d4 24 ♖a3 ♕b6! and Black emerged from the complications with winning chances (0–1, 63).

Another interesting sidelight on the question of Sicilians with ... e5 is the following line of the Taimanov variation: 1 e4 c5 2 ♘f3 e6 (or 2 ... ♘c6) 3 d4 cd 4 ♘×d4 ♘c6 5 ♘b5 d6 6 ♗f4 (6 c4! is another story.) 6 ... e5 7 ♗e3 *(6)* – a position that can easily lead to confusion with the Lasker variation. This sequence must also be distinguished from that in the Four Knights' variation, which really does transpose to the main line of the Lasker but with a tempo lost by each player: 1 e4 c5 2 ♘f3 ♘c6 3 d4 cd 4 ♘×d4 ♘f6 5 ♘c3 e6 6 ♘db5 d6 (6 ... ♗b4 7 a3±) 7 ♗f4 e5 8 ♗g5 a6 etc.

Now, in this position from his own variation, Taimanov normally played 7 ... ♘f6 8 ♗g5 (8 ♘1c3 see chapter 4, D23) 8 ... ♗e6 (8 ... ♕a5+? 9 ♕d2!±) 9 ♘1c3 a6 10 ♗×f6 gf 11 ♘a3. Comparison with chapter 5 shows White to be a tempo down as White has moved his queen's bishop three times while the black e-pawn only moved twice. The first Fischer–Petrosian match game, 1971, showed the best way to handle this position: 11 ... d5! (akin to Pelikan's idea) 12 ed ♗×a3 13 ba ♕a5 14 ♕d2 OOO! (making use of the extra tempo) 15 ♗c4 ♖hg8 16 ♖d1! and now, as many commentators indicated, 16 ... ♖×g2! would have given Black a virtually winning position. However,

a natural improvement for White is 9 ♘d2!, heading for c4 and leaving c3 free for the ♘b5.

Another attempt to improve upon the Lasker variation is to play 7 ... a6 from diagram 6 (not 7 ... ♗e6 8 c4 – Holmov). Then after 8 ♘5c3 ♘f6 White could again transpose to the line on page 48 by 9 ♘a3, but this gives him nothing, while 9 ♗c4 (or 9 ♗e2 ♗e7 10 00 00 11 ♘d2 b5!=) 9 ... ♘a5 (9 ... ♗e7? 10 ♘d5!) 10 ♗d5 ♗e6 11 ♕d3 ♖c8 12 ♘d2 ♘b4 is also satisfactory for Black (following Nikitin). The critical lines, after 9 ♗g5 ♗e7, are:

a) 10 ♗×f6 ♗×f6 11 ♘d5 ♗g5! 12 ♗c4 00 13 00 ♗e6 14 ♗b3 ♗h6 15 ♘1c3 ♔h8 16 ♕d3 ♖c8 17 ♖ad1 ♕h4 18 f3 ♘d4= Kapengut-Tal, USSR 1965

b) 10 ♘d2 ♗e6 11 ♘c4 ♗×c4 12 ♗×c4 00 13 ♗e3 ♖c8 (Estrin-Ljungdahl, corres 1971–2) 14 ♗b3 – *Fernschach*, 1972.

To conclude, all the lines with ... e5 in this book can be played as part of an aggressive opening repertoire for Black. There are certain risks involved in the 4 ... e5 and 5 ... e5 variations, since it is impossible to be sure that there is not a way for White to get an advantage in the main lines. However, most active defences share this element of dangerous excitement. It is anyway not so easy for White to find good moves over the board, and even if he gets a slight positional advantage (±), sophisticated endgame play will often be needed to exploit it. Black's main chances lie in the cut-and-thrust of middle game tactics, often involving sacrifices to get the initiative, and experience shows that he thereby gets a good proportion of wins – at least in amateur chess, and in the case of 5 ... e5 at master level too. We should like to end by emphasizing that in many cases there are strong moves and new plans waiting to be discovered for both players, so that home analysis based on this book is likely to pay dividends.

# 1  4 ... e5, 8 ♛d1

Is the La Bourdonnais Variation sound? Theory and practice both suggest that the crux of the matter lies in the assessment of the position which arises from 1 e4 c5 2 ♘f3 ♘c6 3 d4 cd 4 ♘ × d4 e5!? 5 ♘b5 a6 6 ♘d6+ ♗ × d6 7 ♛ × d6 ♛f6 8 ♛d1 (7).

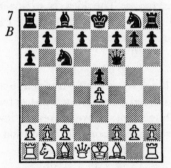

Black has given up the two bishops, and is left with a pattern of weak black squares around his king, and a backward d-pawn. His active chances lie mostly on the white squares, using his queen from g6 to attack White's e-pawn and g-pawn and following up with a ... d5 pawn sacrifice in many cases. White's 8 ♛d1 was not the only good retreat (see

chapter two for the others), but it has been the most popular since its introduction by Gligorić in 1957. On d1, the queen keeps out of trouble, does not obstruct her own minor pieces and protects the c-pawn. In addition, she keeps a watch on d5.

Black's task is therefore to turn his slight lead in development into some concrete gain before White can consolidate his grip on d5 and the black squares. The play can become very sharp as Black seeks to avoid an inferior endgame.

8 ...                    ♛g6

8 ... ♘ge7 9 ♘c3 00!? (9 ... ♛g6 below) needs more tests. After 10 ♗e3:

a) **10 ... d6** 11 ♛d2 b5 12 000 ♖d8 13 ♚b1 ♛g6 14 f3 (14 f4!? ef 15 ♗ × f4 ♗g4!= – V) 14 ... ♗b7 (14 ... ♗e6 15 ♘d5± Gligorić – Rossetto, Santa Fe 1960) 15 g4! f6 16 ♘d5 ♘ × d5 17 ♛ × d5±± Gligorić – Benko, Dublin 1957.

b) **10 ... b5** 11 ♛d2 ♛g6 12 f3 d5!? (12 ... d6 see a) when V gives:

b1) **13 ed?** ♘b4 14 000 ♖d8!

b2) **13 ♘ × d5** ♘ × d5 14 ♕ × d5
(14 ed ♘d4 15 ♗d3 ♗f5) 14 ...
♖d8 15 ♕c5 ♗b7 is unclear (16
♕b6? ♘b4!).

9 ♘c3            ♘ge7(*8*)

Not 9 ... ♘f6?! 10 ♕d6! ♘g4
11 ♕ × g6 hg 12 ♘d5! ±

Black intends to play ... d5
next if he can, and after the capture ed (♘ × d5 generally allows
... ♕ × e4+) he has ... ♘b4,
threatening the white c-pawn
with check, while the ♗c8 is also
freed to come out to f5. Note that
the presence of the black queen at
g6 makes it hard for White to
develop his king's bishop, and if
he wants to arrange Q-side castling he will eventually have to
move his queen again.

The brightest spot on the
horizon for White is that Black's
sacrifice will create a mobile
passed d-pawn that can be used to
harass the black king. There will
also be occasions where White can
allow Black to play ... ♕ × g2.
Many games with the La Bourdonnais Variation are effectively
decided in the next four or five

moves, so it is very important that
White should take the right
decisions now.

We look at:

A 10 f3
B 10 ♗e3
C 10 h4!

Popovsky–Ushakov, Ukraine
Corres Ch 1961–5, went instead
10 g3?! d5 11 ♗g2 de 12 ♘ × e4
00∓. Black threatened 13 ... ♖d8
and 14 ... ♘d4, so White dared
not castle but played 13 c3
instead; 13 ... ♗h3! was the
reply, and Black won in 37 moves.

**A**

**10 f3**

Pachman once recommended
this move. The idea is to meet
10 ... d5? by 11 ♘ × d5, since e4
is now protected.

10 ...            00
11 ♗e3            d5!

Black refuses to be trapped in a
positional game. The tempo lost by
White's tenth move makes the in-
vestment a reasonable proposition.

12 ♘ × d5        ♘ × d5
13 ♕ × d5        ♖d8!

Matulović–Gerusel, Halle 1967,
went 13 ... ♗e6 14 ♕d2 ♖ad8
15 ♕f2 f5 16 ef ♗ × f5 17 c3 e4
18 f4 ♗e6 19 ♗e2 ♘e5 20 00
♘d3 21 ♕h4!±.

14 ♕c4            ♗e6
15 ♕e2            f5
16 ef            ♗ × f5

Black is a tempo ahead of the
previous note. Bogdanović–Minić,
Bled 1963, concluded 17 ♕f2 (17

c3 ♗d3) 17 ... ♗×c2 18 ♗c4+
♔h8 19 00 ♗d3 20 ♗×d3
♖×d3 ½–½.

**B**

### 10 ♗e3

White goes for development
and allows Black his gambit.

10 ...　　　　d5!(9)

10 ... 00 is less consistent.
Milić–de Rooi, Amsterdam 1963,
continued 11 a3 (to prevent
... ♘b4; 11 ♗c5!?) 11 ... d5 12
ed ♘d4 13 ♗×d4 ed 14 ♕×d4
♕×c2 15 ♗d3 ♕×b2 16 00
♘f5 17 ♕c5 ♕c2 18 ♖fd1 ♕c4
19 ♖ab1 b5 20 ♖bc1±.

B1 11 ed
B2 11 ♘×d5

**B1**

### 11 ed　　　　♘b4
12 ♗d3

White hasn't much choice in
view of 12 ♖c1 ♗f5, e.g. 13 d6
♖d8 14 ♕f3 ♕×d6 (0–1, 52)
Gurfinkel–Strelnikova,　　USSR
Spartakiad 1975.

After 12 ♗d3:

B11 12 ... ♗f5
B12 12 ... ♘×d3+!

**B11**

### 12 ...　　　　♗f5
13 ♗×f5

Not 13 00? when:

a) **13 ... ♗×d3** 14 cd ♘b×d5
15 ♘×d5 ♘×d5 16 ♗c5 ♘f4
17 ♕f3 ♕c6 18 ♕×c6 bc 19
♖ad1 000 20 d4 ed (0–1, 40)
Suyagin – Venglovsky,　corres
1961–5; or

b) **13 ... ♖c8** 14 ♗×f5 ♘×f5
15 ♖c1 ♖×c3! 16 bc ♘×a2 17
♖a1 ♘h4 18 g3 ♕e4!∓∓ (19
gh ♘×c3 wins the queen); Luik–
Kliavin, Vilnius 1959.

13 ...　　　　♘×f5
14 ♗c5!

Better than 14 00:

a) **14 ... ♘×e3** 15 fe ♘×c2 16
♖c1 ♘×e3 17 ♕e2 ♘×f1 18
♕×e5+:

a1) **18 ... ♔d8?** 19 d6! ♕e6 20
♕a5+ ♔e8 21 ♘d5!± Kothe–
Baumbach, E. Germany 1967

a2) **18 ... ♔d7** 19 ♖×f1 ♖ae8
would have been a better test of
White's exchange sacrifice, e.g.
20 ♕f4 (or 20 ♕d4 ♔c7!) 20 ...
♕b6+ 21 ♔h1 f6 – CMQ.

b) **14 ... ♘h4** is also playable,
e.g. 15 g3 ♘×c2 16 ♖c1 ♘×e3
17 fe 00 18 ♔h1 ♘f5 – CMQ.

14 ...　　　　♕×g2

Baumbach's recommendation
14 ... ♘d4?! fails to 15 ♗×b4
(He only considered 15 00.) 15
♘×c2+　16　♔f1　♘×b4　17
♕a4+ etc. – V. If 15 ... ♕×g2
16 ♖f1 ♘f3+ see below.

15 ♖f1　　　　♘h4

16 ♗×b4    ♘f3+
17 ♔e2    ♕g4
18 h3!±±

Hennings–Baumbach, E. German Ch 1963; White was able to hold on to his extra piece. If 18 ... ♘g1+ (18 ... ♘d4+ 19 ♔d3) 19 ♔d2! ♕f4+ 20 ♔e1 ♘f3+ 21 ♔e2 ♘d4+ 22 ♔d3 etc.

**B12**

12 ...          ♘×d3+!(10)

13 ♕×d3

Or 13 cd!? when:

a) CMQ gives 13 ... ♕×g2 14 ♕a4+ ♗d7 15 ♕e4± (passed pawn).

b) 13 ...♗f5 is promising, e.g.:

b1) 14 ♕a4+ b5! 15 ♘×b5 00 with strong threats, or

b2) 14 00 00! and Black will safely regain his pawn – Harding and Povah.

13 ...          ♗f5!?

13 ... ♕×d3 14 cd ♗f5 may be better:

a) 15 ♖d1 ♖d8= Bertok–Minić, Bled 1963

b) 15 d6!? ♘c8 (15 ... ♘c6 16 ♘d5 00 17 ♖d1 ♖d8 18 ♗c5±)
16 ♗c5 ♔d7 17 ♘e4 ♖d8 and Black regains his pawn soon – V.

14 ♕d2

A critical position, in which Black has several options, although none may be wholly satisfactory.

14 ...          00

Others:

a) 14 ... ♗×c2!? 15 00 ♖d8 (15 ... 00 16 ♗c5 ♖fe8 17 ♖fe1 f6 below) 16 ♗c5 ♕d3 17 ♕g5! ♘g6 18 ♖fe1 f6 19 ♕g4 ♕f5 with a tenable but hardly inspiring position; O'Hara–Rossetto, Varna 1962;

b) 14 ... ♕×g2 (= – G) 15 000 with a very sharp game. White's chances seem preferable as the black queen is decentralised and the g-file may become an avenue for white rooks.

c) 14 ... ♖c8!? is interesting, but probably favours White after 15 00! (Castling Q-side is asking for trouble.) 15 ... ♗×c2 (15 ... 00 16 f4!) 16 d6 (Not 16 ♖ac1 ♗d3 17 ♖fe1 e4 intending ... ♘f5) 16 ... ♖d8 17 ♖ac1 ♗e4 (or 17·... ♗f5 18 ♗c5 ♘c8 19 ♘d5 ♘×d6 20 ♘c7+ ♔e7 21 ♖fe1) 18 ♘×e4 ♕×e4 19 ♗b6! ♖d7 20 ♕g5! ♖×d6 21 ♗c5 ♖d7 22 ♗×e7 ♖×e7 23 ♖c8+ etc. – Harding and Povah.

15 ♗c5!

Not 15 00 ♖fd8 when:

a) 16 f4 ef 17 ♖×f4 ♗×c2 18 ♖c1 ♗d3 (0–1, 53) Schulten-

Heidrich, The Hague 1975 – not a very convincing game;

b) **16 ♗c5** ♘×d5! regains the pawn, because of 17 ♘×d5 ♖×d5! 18 ♕×d5 ♗e4 threatening mate.

15 ...        ♖fe8
16 00        ♗×c2

Not 16 ... ♖ac8 (nor 16 ... ♖ad8 17 ♖fe1±) 17 ♗×e7 ♖×e7 18 ♖fe1 ♗×c2 19 d6 ♖d7 20 ♖ac1 ♗f5 21 ♘d5± – Harding and Povah

17 ♖fe1      f6

a) **18 f4** ♖ac8 19 ♗×e7 ♖×e7 20 d6 ♖d7 21 ♖ac1 ♗f5 22 ♘d5 ♖cd8 23 ♖c7 ♔h8 24 ♘e7 ♕e8! forcing simplifications ($\frac{1}{2}-\frac{1}{2}$, 44) Janošević–Matulović, Maribor 1967; Black was probably lucky here.

b) **18 d6!?** is also critical, e.g. 18 ... ♘c6 19 ♘d5 ♖ed8 (19 ... ♖ad8 20 ♘c7 ♖f8 21 ♘e6) 20 ♗b6 ♖d7. Can Black survive?
**B2**

    **11 ♘×d5**    ♘×d5

11 ... ♕×e4 is not check here, so it loses to 12 ♘c7+.

    12 ♕×d5

Not 12 ed? ♘b4 13 ♔d2 (13 ♖c1 ♗f5∓) 13 ... ♗f5 14 c4 b5! 15 b3 bc 16 bc 00∓ Aalders–Ditt, Beverwijk 1958.

12 ...        ♗e6!?*(11)*

12 ... 00! has been less played:

a) **13 ♕d2** ♕×e4 14 f3 ♕g6 15 ♗d3 ♗f5 16 ♗×f5 ♕×f5(∓–U) 17 00 ♖ad8 (=CMQ) Cirić–Szabo, Belgrade 1964

b) CMQ suggests **13 f3**, transposing to A.

*11*
*W*

    13 ♕d2

This is much better than 13 ♕c5? (13 ♕d3? ♖d8) 13 ... ♕×e4 14 000 (14 c3 ♖d8= Ostojić–Basman, Hastings 1967–8) 14 ... ♖c8 15 ♗d3 ♕a4 16 a3 ♘d4 17 ♕b4 ♖×c2+ 18 ♔b1 ♕×b4∓ Unzicker–Mandel, W. German Ch 1959.

13 ...        ♕×e4
14 f3        ♕d5

Others:

a) **14 ...** ♕a4 15 ♗d3 00 16 a3 ♘d4 17 00 ♖fd8 18 ♕f2 ♖ac8 19 ♖ad1 ♗c4 (Foguelman–Rossetto, Mar del Plata 1965) deserves further tests.

b) **14 ...** ♕h4+ 15 g3! ♕e7:

b1) **16 ♕f2** ♘d4! Dückstein–Andersson, Raach 1969

b2) **16 ♗g2** 00 17 00 ♖ac8 18 c3 ♘a5 19 b3 b5 20 c4 ♘b7 21 cb ab 22 ♕e2 ♘d6 23 ♖fc1± Cirić–Zinn, Mariánské Lazné 1962.

15 ♕×d5      ♗×d5
16 ♗b6!

Still more effective than 16 000

000 17 ♗b6± of Möhring–Baumbach, E. German Team Ch 1964.

| | |
|---|---|
| 16 ... | ♘b4 |
| 17 ♔d2 | ♗e6 |
| 18 c4 | f6 |

19 ♔c3 ♘c6 20 ♗d3 ♖c8 21 b3 ♘e7 22 ♔b2 and according to CMQ 'Black has to struggle against considerable odds'; Zinn–Baumbach, E. German Teams Ch 1963. White has two bishops and a mobile Q-side pawn majority. This is why Black should give preference to 14 ... ♕a4 or to 12 ... 00, avoiding this ending.

**C**

**10 h4!**

As White has little intention of castling K-side, it's worth it for him to try and weaken Black on that side. In this way he gains a better square for his queen's bishop without loss of time, since Black must try to maintain his queen on its active square, g6.

10 ...         h5(*12*)

Not:

a) **10 ... h6** 11 h5 ♕f6 12 ♗e3 00 13 ♕d2 b5 14 000 b4 15 ♘a4 a5 16 ♘b6 ♖b8 17 ♕d6 ♕ × d6 18 ♖ × d6 ± Boleslavsky–Sakharov, Kiev 1957

b) **10 ... d5** 11 h5 ♕d6:

b1) **12 h6!?** g6 13 ed ♘d4 14 ♘e4 Zvorikina–Veisberg, USSR 1957

b2) **12 ed** ♘b4 13 ♗c4 ♗f5 14 ♗b3 ♖d8 15 g4!± Szabo–Szily, Hungarian Ch 1964

c) Can **10 ... f5!?** be played? Two possibilities are:

c1) **11 h5** ♕e6 12 b3 b5 13 a4 fe 14 ab?! ♘d4 15 ♗c4 d5

c2) **11 ♘d5** ♘ × d5 12 ♕ × d5 d6 13 ♗c4!? ♘d4! – Harding and Povah.

*12*
*W*

C1 11 ♖h3
C2 11 ♗g5!

**C1**

**11 ♖h3**

This move leads to great complications.

| | |
|---|---|
| 11 ... | d5! |
| 12 ♖g3 | ♗g4 |

12 ... ♕h7 looks too passive:

a) **13 ed** ♘b4 14 ♗d3 ♗f5 15 d6 ♗ × d3 16 cd ♘f5 17 ♕a4+ ♘c6 18 d7+ ♔ × d7 (Jakobsen–Borja, Tel Aviv 1964) is unclear.

b) **13 ♗e2** d4 14 ♘d5 ♘ × d5 15 ed ♘b4 16 ♖g5!± e.g. 16 ... ♘ × c2+ 17 ♔f1 ♘ × a1 18 ♖ × h5 ♕g8 19 ♖ × e5+ ♔d8 20 ♕ × d4! with an apparently decisive attack – G.

13 f3

Not 13 ♗e2 de! 14 ♗ × g4 ♖d8 15 ♗d2 hg 16 ♕ × g4 e3! 17

♗×e3 ♕×c2∓ Bastrikov-Gufeld, USSR Team Ch 1958.

13 ...          de
14 ♘×e4

If 14 fg?!:

a) Not **14 ... f5?** 15 ♗g5 ♖d8 16 ♕c1 (1-0, 32) Kochiev-Lutikov, Daugavpils 1974

b) but possibly **14 ... ♘f5** (Sokolsky) or

c) **14 ... ♖d8!** 15 ♗d2 f5! e.g.:

c1) **16 g5** f4∓ Bosković-Krstev, Pula 1965

c2) **16 ♖e3?** hg 17 g3 ♘d4∓∓ – B.

c3) **16 ♕c1** hg 17 ♗g5 ♘d4 – G.

14 ...          ♖d8
15 ♗d3          f5
16 ♘c3!

Others:

a) **16 ♘f2** e4 17 fg ed 18 ♖×d3 fg (or 18 ... 00! – V) 19 ♖×d8+ ♘×d8 20 ♗g5 ♘e6 21 ♗×e7 ♔×e7∓ Zhelyandinov-Levin, Odessa 1962

b) **16 ♘g5** e4 17 fg hg! 18 ♘×e4 fe (18 ... ♖×h4? 19 ♘f2) 19 ♖×g4 when:

b1) **19 ... ♕d6** 20 ♖×e4 ♕g3+ 21 ♔d2 00 (Geller-Bronstein, Kislovodsk 1968) was unclear:

b2) **19 ... ♖×h4!?** has been suggested as an improvement, e.g. 20 ♖×g6 ♖h1+ 21 ♔f2 ♖×d1 (21 ♗f1 ♖×d1+ or 21 ♔e2 ed+) 22 ♗×e4 (22 ♗e2 ♖×c1!) 22 ... ♘×g6 23 ♗×g6+ ♔f8 24 b3 b5! 25 c3 ♘e5 26 ♗a3+ ♔g8 and Black's extra exchange begins to tell – AHM.

16 ...          e4
17 fg          hg

Black should probably play 17 ... ed! 18 ♖×d3 00 19 ♗g5 (19 gh ♕×g2 or 19 gf f4!) 19 ... fg e.g. 20 ♗×e7 ♖de8 21 ♖e3 ♘×e7+ – V.

18 ♗g5

The position is so confused that, without deep analysis, one cannot say who stands better. Black must try to improve on the following, not very convincing game: 18 ... ed (18 ... ♕d6!? 19 ♔f2) 19 ♖×d3 ♖×d3 20 ♕×d3 ♕e6+? (20 ... ♔f7!?) 21 ♔f1 ♕d7 22 ♕e2 ♔f7 23 ♖e1 ♖e8 24 ♕c4+ ♔f8 25 ♖e6! b5?? (25 ... ♘g8 26 ♖×e8+ ♕×e8 27 ♕c5+ ♘ge7 28 ♘d5!) 26 ♖f6+! gf 27 ♗h6 mate; Mak-Bohak, Hungary v. Yugoslavia corres 1970-1.

## C2

**11 ♗g5!**

White is preparing to trade in his two bishops for an endgame advantage.

11 ...          d5(*13*)

Black is committed to this, in view of:

a) **11 ... d6** 12 ♕d2 00 13 000 ♖d8 14 ♘d5±

b) **11 ... f6** 12 ♗e3 d5 (12 ... 00 looks positionally terrible.) 13 ♘×d5 ♘×d5 14 ♕×d5± since, compared with B2, neither ... ♗e6 nor ... 00 is playable and there is probably nothing better than 14 ... ♕f7 15 ♗c4 with a

very good position for White – K.
c) **11 ... b5** 12 a3 d6 13 ♕d2
again with good prospects for
White on the d-file; Kayumov–
Agzamov, Uzbekistan Ch 1973.

*13*
*W*

C21 12 ♗×e7
C22 12 ed!
**C21**

**12 ♗×e7**     d4!
An important intermediate
move.

13 ♗c5
Others:
a) **13 ♘d5?** ♕×e4+
b) **13 ♘e2?** ♘×e7 14 ♘g3 ♗g4
(14 ... ♕c6!? – V) 15 ♗e2 f5∓
van den Berg–Vlagsma, Holland
1958
c) **13 ♗g5** dc 14 bc ♕×e4+
15 ♗e2:
c1) **15 ... f6** 16 ♗e3 ♗g4 17
♕d3! ♕×d3 (17 ... ♕a4 18
♕g6+) 18 cd ♗×e2 19 ♔×e2
000= Fischer–Tal, Curaçao 1962
c2) In *Europe–Echecs*, Le Monnier
suggested **15 ... ♗f5!?**, meeting
16 ♖c1 by 16 ... f6 17 ♗d2 ♖d8
(e.g. 18 f3 ♕a4∓ – V). This
seems plausible, but White might

blast a way through by 16 00!?
♕×c2 (16 ... f6 17 ♗×h5+)
17 ♕d6!: since
c21) **17 ... ♕×e2** 18 ♖fe1 ♕c4
(but 18 ... ♕g4 looks like a
refutation.) 19 ♖×e5+ ♗e6 20
♖c5! (20 ... ♕e4 21 ♖×c6!)
it's all over; or
c22) **17 ... f6** 18 ♗×f6 gf 19
♕×f6, with a strong attack for
the piece, is critical – Harding
and Povah.

13 ...          dc
14 f3
Or:
a) **14 bc** ♕×e4+ 15 ♕e2 ♗f5
16 ♕×e4 ♗×e4 17 000 ♖d8=
Shianovsky–Baumbach,    Bucharest 1962.
b) **14 ♕d3**:
b1) **14 ... cb** 15 ♖b1 f5 (15 ...
b6!? as in the main line) 16
♖×b2 fe 17 ♕e3 ♗g4 18
♖×b7±± Mukhitdinov – Shah-
zade, USSR 1962.
b2) **14 ... ♗e6!** 15 ♕×c3
♕×e4+ with an unclear position
–Gligorić.

14 ...          cb
15 ♖b1          b6!
Or:
a) **15 ... ♕g3+** 16 ♗f2 ♕g6= –
G; White must either repeat the
position or allow K-side castling.
b) **15 ... ♗e6** 16 ♖×b2 ♖d8 17
♕c1 ♖d7! (17 ... f5? 18 ♖×b7
fe 19 ♗×a6 ef 20 ♗b5) 18 c3 f6
19    ♖b6    ♔f7    20 ♕b2±
Matanović   –   Bouwmeester,
Utrecht 1961.

16 ♗×b6
Not 16 ♗a3 ♕g3+

| 16 ... | 00 |
| 17 ♖×b2 | ♖b8 |

Black has good play for his pawn, e.g.:

a) **18 ♖b1** ♖×b6! 19 ♖×b6 ♕g3+ – CMQ.

b) **18 ♔f2** ♗e6! with great complications in store – AHM.

## C22

**12 ed!** (*14*)

14
B

C221 12 ... ♘d4?
C222 12 ... ♘b4

## C221

**12 ...        ♘d4?**

Originally suggested by Euwe.

| 13 ♗d3 | ♗f5 |
| 14 ♗×f5 | |

14 00 is not so clear, although Winiwarter–N. Littlewood, Tel Aviv, Olympiad 1964, continued 14 ... f6 15 ♗e3 ♗×d3 16 cd 00 17 ♗×d4 ed 18 d6 ♘f5 19 ♘d5±.

14 ...        ♘e×f5

Or 14 ... ♕×f5 15 00 f6 16 ♗e3 ♘×c2 17 ♖c1 ♘×e3 18 fe:

a) **18 ...** ♕d7? 19 d6 ♘c6 20 ♘d5 00 21 ♖×c6! 1–0 Strautins–Norkin, corres 1972.

b) **18 ...** ♕g4 19 ♕×g4 (19 ♕b3 ♘f5! 20 ♕×b7 00) 19 ... hg 20 g3± thanks to the passed d-pawn – K.

| 15 ♕d3! | f6 |
| 16 ♗e3 | ♕g4 |

16 ... ♕×g2 17 000 e.g.:

a) **17 ...** ♕f3 18 ♘e4 00 19 c3 ♘e2+ 20 ♔b1 ♘f4 21 ♗×f4 ♕×d3+ 22 ♖×d3 ef 23 ♘c5 ♘d6 24 ♘e6 ♖f7 25 ♘×f4±± Sakharov–Shianovsky, Ukraine Ch 1962.

b) **17 ...** 000 18 ♘e4 intending 19 c3 – R.

| 17 ♗×d4 | ed |

Sokolsky and R suggested 17 ... ♘×d4, but then 18 ♘e2 ♕×g2 19 000 ♕×d5 20 ♔b1! (threatening 21 c3) e.g.:

a) **20 ...** ♕f7 21 ♘×d4 ed 22 ♖he1+ is very difficult for Black; or

b) **20 ...** ♕c5 21 ♕g6+ ♔f8 22 ♘×d4 ed 23 ♖hg1 ♖g8 24 c3! ♖d8 (24 ... dc 25 ♖d7 c2+ 26 ♔c1) 25 cd ♖×d4 26 ♖c1 ♖c4 27 ♕d3! b5 28 b3±± – K.

| 18 ♘e2 | ♕×g2 |
| 19 000 | ♕×f2 |
| 20 ♔b1!±± | |

Vasyukov–Malich, Berlin 1962. White threatens 21 ♖hf1, now that he has avoided the check on e3. There is no good defence:

a) **20 ...** ♘e3 21 ♕g6+ ♔f8 22 ♘×d4!

b) **20 ...** g6 21 ♕e4+ ♔f7 22 d6.

**C222**

**12 ...**   **♘b4**(15)

15
W

C2221 13 ♗d3
C2222 13 ♖c1
C2223 13 ♗×e7!

13 d6 ♘ec6 14 ♗d3 ♘×d3+ 15 ♕×d3 ♗f5 (15 ... ♕×d3!? – V) 16 d7+ ♚f8 17 ♕d5 f6 18 ♗e3 ♕f7 19 000 ♖d8= Nikitin-Gufeld, Tbilisi 1959.

**C2221**

**13 ♗d3**   **♘×d3+**

13 ... ♗f5!? may be playable.

14 ♕×d3

Not 14 cd f6 15 d6 ♘c6 16 ♘d5 00 17 ♖c1 ♖f7∓ Conrady-Belkadi, Varna Olympiad 1962.

14 ...   ♗f5

14 ... ♕×d3 15 cd f6 is comparable with C22232, but probably with more drawing chances for Black.

15 ♕c4

If 15 ♕f3 (or 15 ♕d2) 15 ...f6 positions with similarities to B12 arise, but with Black benefiting somewhat from the advance of the h-pawns.

15 ...   f6

16 ♗e3   ♖c8

Necessary, if Black is ever to castle. Now:

a) Levy-Povah, Herts v. Surrey 1975, continued **17 ♕a4+?!** b5! 18 ♕×a6 00 19 ♕×b5 (19 ♕d6 ♕×g2 20 000 ♖×c3! 21 bc ♕e4∓∓) 19 ... ♖b8! 20 ♕c5 ♖×b2 21 d6 (21 ♕×e7? ♕×g2) 21 ... ♕×g2 22 ♖f1 (22 de ♕×h1+ 23 ♚e2 ♖×c2+ 24 ♗d2 ♗g4+ 25 ♚d3 ♖×c3+∓) 22 ... ♘c6! 23 ♕d5+ ♕×d5 24 ♘×d5 ♖×c2 25 ♖c1 ♖×c1+ 26 ♗×c1 ♖a8 27 ♖g1 ♚f7 28 ♘c3 ♘b4 29 a4 ♖a6 30 ♚e2 ♖×d6 31 ♗a3 ♖d4 32 ♖d1 ♖×h4 33 a5 ♗g4+ 34 f3 ♖h2+ 35 ♚f1 ♗×f3 36 ♖d7+ ♚e6 37 ♖×g7 ♘d3 38 a6 ♖c2 39 ♘b5 ♖a2 40 ♖e7+ ♚f5 0-1.

b) The critical line here is **17 ♕b3!** ♗×c2 (17 ... ♕×g2? 18 000 and 19 d6) 18 ♕×b7 ♕×g2 (18 ... ♕d3?! 19 ♖c1±±) 19 ♚d2 (19 ♖f1? ♗d3) when Povah intended 19 ... ♕g6 e.g.:
b1) **20 d6** ♕d3+ 21 ♚c1 00!? 22 de ♖fe8 (threatening 23 ... ♗a4) 23 a4 ♖c4 when it is unclear whether Black's bind compensates sufficiently for the material sacrificed; or
b2) **20 ♖hg1** ♕d3+ 21 ♚e1 ♖×c3 22 bc ♕×c3+ 23 ♚e2 ♕d3+ draws – V.

**C2222**

**13 ♖c1**

This was the main line until Baumbach showed the correct

way for Black to handle the position.

    13 ...         f6!

The 'obvious' 13 ... ♗f5 is well met by 14 d6!, viz.:

a) **14 ... f6** 15 de fg 16 ♕f3 e4 17 ♕e3 gh 18 ♖×h4 ♖c8 19 ♖f4± Bobkov–Beleyev, USSR 1962.

b) **14 ...** ♘×c2+ 15 ♖×c2! ♗×c2 16 ♕d2 ♘c6 (16 ... f6 17 de fg 18 ♖h3! – Fuchs) 17 d7+ ♔f8 18 ♕d8=♕+ ♘×d8 19 ♗×d8± Romanovsky–Lenchiner Odessa 1959.

    14 a3

If 14 d6 ♘ec6, or 14 ♗e3 ♗f5 (15 d6 ♖d8).

    14 ...         fg

    15 hg

15 ab is risky in view of 15 ... gh 16 ♖×h4:

a) **16 ...** ♗**g4** 17 ♕d2 ♖d8 (Durao – Cuartas, Cienfuegos 1975) is unclear;

b) **16 ...** ♘**f5** 17 ♖h2 ♘d4 18 ♗d3 ♗f5 19 ♘e2 000 20 ♘g3 e4 21 ♗c4 h4 22 ♘f1 ♘c6∓ Jansa–Baumbach, Bad Liebenstein 1963.

    15 ...         ♗g4!

    16 ♕d2         ♘b×d5

    17 ♘×d5         ♘×d5

    18 ♕×d5         ♕×g5

White has no significant advantage. Fuchs–Baumbach, from a later round of Bad Liebenstein 1963, continued: 19 ♕d2 ♕×d2+ 20 ♔×d2 ♔e7 21 ♗d3 ♖ad8 22 ♔e3 h4 23 g3 (23 ♖h2 b5= Liebert–Baumbach, E. German Ch 1963) 23 ... hg 24 ♖×h8 ♖×h8 25 ♖g1 ♖h3 26 ♖×g3 ♖×g3+ 27 fg a5 ½–½.

**C2223**

    **13 ♗×e7!**    ♔×e7 *(16)*

Not 13 ... ♘×c2+ 14 ♔d2 ♘×a1 15 d6± – Milić, *Informator* 6.

*16 W*

C22231 14 d6+!?
C22232 14 ♗d3

**C22231**

    **14 d6+!?**    ♔d8!

Better than 14 ... ♕×d6 15 ♕×d6+ ♔×d6 16 000+ when:

a) 16 ... ♔c7 17 a3 ♘c6 18 ♘d5+ ♔b8 19 ♘b6 ♖a7 20 ♗c4 ♖f8 21 ♖d7±± Begun–Korolyev, USSR 1966.

b) 16 ... ♔e7 17 a3± – Milić. This does look a bit annoying for Black, although Le Monnier thought that Black could put up a fair resistance by 17 ... ♘c6 followed by 18 ... ♗e6, or in some cases 18 ... f6.

    15 ♖c1?

Better 15 ♗d3 when:

a) **15 ...** ♘×**d3**+ 16 ♕×d3 ♕×d3 17 cd:

a1) **17 ...** ♗**f5** 18 ♘d5!? (18 000

♔d7 19 d4 e4 20 ♖he1± – U –
20 ... ♖ad8±) 18 ... ♖h6 19
♘b6 ♖b8 20 00 ♖×d6 21 ♘c4
♖d4 22 ♘×e5 f6 23 ♘f3 ♖×d3
½-½ Miles–Povah, Manchester
1972.

a2) **17 ... ♖h6!**= Karsa–
Streitberg, Budapest v. Prague
1972.

b) 15 ... ♗f5!? 16 ♗×f5 ♕×f5
is a way for Black to play for a
win at some risk, e.g. 17 00!
♘×c2 18 ♖c1 ♘d4 19 ♘a4? (19
f4! is critical.) 19 ... ♖h6 20
♘b6? ♖g6! 21 ♘×a8? ♘f3+
22 ♔h1 ♖×g2!∓∓ – K.

    15 ...          ♗f5

Or 15 ... ♗g4 16 ♕d2 ♖h6
(16 ... ♗f5 17 ♘d5!) 17 a3
♘c6 18 ♗c4 ♘d4 19 ♕g5+
forcing a very good ending for
White, e.g. 19 ... f6 20 ♕×g6
♖×g6 21 ♗f7 ♖h6 22 ♗d5±
Kupreichik–Georgiev, Student
Olympiad, Ybbs 1968.

    16 ♕f3

A critical position. Who is
right?:

a) **16 ... ♖b8?** 17 ♗c4! ♘×c2+
18 ♖×c2 ♗×c2 19 00±± e.g.
19 ... ♖f8 20 ♖c1 ♗f5 21 ♕e3
threatening both 22 ♕b6+ and
22 ♕×e5 – B.

b) **16 ... ♖c8** 17 ♕×b7 ♕×d6
18 ♗×a6! ♖b8 19 ♕×f7 ♖f8
20 ♕×g7 ♘×c2+ 21 ♖×c2
♗×c2 22 00±± – B.

c) **16 ... ♕h6!** and if 17 ♘e2 (17
♕e3 ♘×c2+) 17 ... ♗×c2∓ –
G. Rastyan in *Sahs* 1974/1. In

view of possible continuations like
18 ♖×c2 ♘×c2+ 19 ♔d1 ♖c8
(threatening 20 ... ♕×d6+), it
looks as if the Latvian amateur
has found a big hole in grandmaster Boleslavsky's analysis;
note that U gives ± after White's
16th move!

**C22232**

    14 ♗d3(17)

    14 ...          ♘×d3+

14 ... ♗f5 15 ♗×f5 ♕×f5 is
dubious because of 16 00 ♘×c2
(else White plays a3) 17 ♖c1
♘d4 18 f4! e.g. 18 ... ♕g4 19 fe
♕×h4 20 ♕d2+ – K.

    15 ♕×d3          ♕×d3

Both 15 ... ♗f5 16 ♕e3 and 15
... ♕×g2 16 000 give White
excellent attacking chances. In
view of his insecure king position,
Black must exchange queens.

    16 cd          b5

As suggested by Baumbach.
Others:

a) **16 ... ♖d8** 17 000 b5 transposes.

b) **16 ... f5!?** (to control e4) 17
000 ♔f6 (17 ... ♔d6 18 d4! e4 19

♖h3±) 18 ♖he1 b5 19 f3 (19 d4
e4 20 f3 ef) 19 ... b4 20 ♘a4 ♗b7
21 d4 ♖c8+ 22 ♔b1 e4 23 fe fe
24 ♘b6± – K.

17 000!

Baumbach only considered 17
a3 ♖b8 18 b4 ♗b7 19 000 ♖ac8
20 ♔b2 ♖fd8 21 ♖he1 (or 21 d4
♗×d5=) 21 ... f6=.

17 ...                    ♖d8

Not 17 ... b4? 18 ♘e4 f5? (18
... ♖d8±) as the game Zuckerman–Bleiman, Netanya 1971,
demonstrated: 19 ♘g5 ♖d8 20 d4
♖×d5 21 de! ♖×e5 22 ♖he1
♖×e1 23 ♖×e1+ ♔f8 24 ♘e6+
♔f7 25 ♘g5+ ♔f8 26 ♖e5! ♖a7
27 ♖c5 (27 ♔c2!?) 27 ... ♗d7
28 ♔d2 ♔e7 29 ♔e3 ♔d6 30
♔d4 ♗c6 31 f3 ♖e7 32 ♖e5!
♖×e5 33 ♘f7+ ♔e6 34 ♘×e5
♗b5 35 f4 ♗f1 36 g3 ♔d6 37
♘c4+ ♔c6 38 ♘e3 ♗h3 39 ♔c4

a5 40 b3 g6 41 ♔d4 ♔b5 1–0
(42 ♔d5 ♔b6 43 ♔e6 ♔c5 44
♔e5! ♔b6 45 ♔f6 – Zuckerman).

18 ♖he1± – Zuckerman

White clearly has the better
ending, but Black is not without
counter-chances.

Conclusion

In the 10 h4 line, the ♕b3
improvement in Levy–Povah
(C2221) is unclear, while there is
no safe way for Black to avoid a
somewhat inferior endgame in
C22232; but 10 ♗e3 d5 11 ed,
though dangerous, can probably
be coped with in the note to
Black's 13th in B12. It is worth
looking for new concepts for
Black, possibly with 10 h4 f5!?, or
by avoiding ... d5 as in our
suggested improvement on
Gligorić–Benko on page 1.

# 2  4 ... e5, 8 Others

All lines in this chapter stem from 1 e4 c5 2 ♞f3 ♞c6 3 d4 cd 4 ♞×d4 e5!? 5 ♞b5 a6 6 ♞d6+ ♝×d6 7 ♛×d6 ♛f6(*18*). In chapter one, we saw how the most popular continuation, 8 ♛d1, leads either to various obscure complications or else, with 'objectively best play' (line C22222) to an endgame which favours White, but not decisively so. White has tried a number of other queen moves in the attempt to establish a clear-cut refutation of the La Bourdonnais Variation, but there is no consensus about which is White's best plan.

A 8 ♛×f6
B 8 ♛d3

18
W

C 8 ♛d2
D 8 ♛c7
E 8 ♛d3

**A**

   **8 ♛×f6**      ♞×f6
    9 ♞c3       d5!?

Others:

a) **9 ... ♞e7** is too passive, e.g. 10 ♝g5 h6?! 11 ♝×f6 gf 12 000± Bubnov–Vasyukin, Moscow 1960.

b) **9 ... ♞b4!** is simplest:

b1) **10 ♚d1** ♞g4 (10 ... d5 11 a3±) 11 ♝e3 ♞×e3+ 12 fe d6 13 a3 ♞c6 14 ♞d5 00 (safer 14 ... ♜b8= – G) 15 ♞b6 ♜b8 16 ♝c4 ♝g4+ 17 ♚d2±.

b2) **10 ♝d3** ♞×d3+ (or 10 ... d5 11 a3 de=) 11 cd h6! (11 ... d5?! 12 ♝g5!± – U) 12 ♝e3 (12 00 d6 13 f4± Kagan – Povah, Hastings 1975/6) 12 ... d6 13 d4 ♝e6 (13 ... ♞g4!? – V) 14 000 ♜c8 (CMQ) 15 ♚b1 00 16 f3 ♜c7= – U.

    10 ♝g5

Or 10 ed!? ♞b4 11 ♝d3 ♞×d3+ 12 cd ♝f5 13 00 000 14 ♝g5 ♝×d3 15 ♜fe1± – U.

    10 ...        d4

a) **10 ...** ♘**b4** 11 ♗×f6 gf 12 ♘d5
♘×c2+ 13 ♔d2 ♘×a1 14
♘c7+ ♔e7 15 ♘×a8 ♗e6 16
♘b6 ♗×a2 17 ♔c3 ♗e6 18 ♗c4
♗×c4 19 ♘×c4 ♖c8 20 ♖×a1
b5 21 b3± Bikhovsky–Minić,
Belgrade 1963.

b) **10 ...** ♘×**e4!** 11 ♘×d5 and
now:

b1) **11 ...** **00** 12 ♗e3 ♖d8 13
♘b6± Toran–Padevsky, Student
Olympiad, Uppsala 1956.

b2) **11 ...** ♘×**g5!?** 12 ♘c7+
♔d7! 13 ♘×a8 ♘b4 with compensation for the exchange – U.
This transposes to:

b3) **11 ...** ♘**b4** 12 ♗d3! (12
♘c7+ ♔d7!) 12 ... ♘×g5 (12
... ♘×d5 13 ♗×e4) 13 ♘c7+
♔d7 14 ♘×a8 e4 (We suggest
14 ... ♔c6!) 15 a3! ed 16 ab
♖e8+ 17 ♔d1!± – G. White's
problem in these lines is how to
extricate his ♘a8.

    11 ♗×f6    dc
    12 ♗×g7    ♖g8
    13 ♗h6!

Not 13 ♗f6? cb 14 ♖b1 ♖g6
15 ♗h4 ♖g4!∓ Klein–Rossetto,
Santa Fe 1960.

    13 ...    cb

For if 13 ... ♘b4 14 000!
♘×a2+ 15 ♔b1 ♗e6 16 ♖d6
♖g6 17 ♗e3 ♘b4 18 ♗c5 and
White will win a pawn – G.

    14 ♖b1±

Cirić – Damjanović, Reggio
Emilia 1966–7, continued 14 ...
♗e6 15 ♖×b2 000 16 ♗e3 ♖d7
17 f3 (17 ♗b6!?) 17 ... ♘a5 18

♖g1 b5 19 a4 ♘c4 20 ♗×c4
♗×c4 21 ♔f2 ♖g6 ½–½, but
White still had the edge at the
end.

**B**

    **8 ♕d3**(*19*)

*19*
*B*

    8 ...    ♘ge7
    9 ♘c3

a) Not: **9 c4** 00 10 ♘c3 d6 11 ♗e2
♕g6 12 00 ♘d4 13 f3 b5∓ Raag–
Agzamov, USSR 1970.

b) **9 g3?** d5! 10 ♗g2 de∓ – V.

    9 ...    d5!

Others:

a) **9 ...** ♕**g6?** 10 ♕g3!

b) **9 ...** ♘**b4?!** 10 ♕d1 ♕g6
(Dückstein–Alster, Wageningen
1957) 11 a3!± – CMQ.

c) **9 ... 00** is important:

c1) **10 a3** ♕g6 11 ♗e3 d5! 12 ed
♗f5 13 ♕d2 ♘d4 14 000 ♘×c2
15 g4!? ♘×e3 16 gf ♘3×f5 17
♗d3 ♖ac8 18 ♗c2 ♖fd8 19
♖hg1 ♕f6∓ Baturinsky –
Antoshin, Moscow 1957.

c2) **10 ♗e3** d5! when:

c21) **11 ed** ♘b4 12 ♕d2 ♗f5 13
♖c1 ♕d6! 14 ♗c4 ♖hd8 15 00
♘b×d5 16 ♗×d5 ♘×d5 17

♕×d5   ♕×d5   18   ♘×d5
♖×d5=   Kolobov – Utyatsky,
Moscow 1962.

c22) **11 ♘×d5** ♘×d5 when:
c221) **12 ed** ♗f5 13 ♕d2 ♘d4
14 ♗d3 ♖ac8 15 c3 ♕g6! 16
♗×f5 ♕×g2 17 ♗×h7+ ♔×h7
18 000 ♕×d5 19 ♗×d4 ed 20
♕d3+ ♔g8 21 ♔b1 ♖fd8= – G.
c222) **12 ♕×d5** ♖d8 13 ♕b3 b5
14 ♗d3 ♕g6 15 g3 ♗g4= – G.

$\qquad$ **10 ♘×d5**

Or 10 ed ♘b4 and 11 ... ♗f5
– CMQ.

**10 ...** $\qquad$ **♘×d5**
**11 ♕×d5**

If 11 ed then 11 ... ♘d4
(Gligorić) or 11 ... ♗f5 12 ♕d2
♘d4 (Euwe).

**11 ...** $\qquad$ **♗e6**
**12 ♕d1**

Euwe gave 12 ♕d2 ♖d8 13
♗d3 ♗c4.

**12 ...** $\qquad$ **♖d8**
**13 ♗d2** $\qquad$ **♕g6!**

This is stronger than 13 ... 00
14 ♗d3 ♕g6 when:
a) **15 ♕f3?** f5 16 ♕g3 ♕f7∓
Vlagsma–Ditt, Beverwijk 1959
b) **15 00** (Euwe) offers White the
better chances of an advantage.

$\qquad$ **14 f3** $\qquad$ **00!**

Black has sufficient compensation for the sacrificed pawn (B);
compare chapter 2, A. A possible
continuation is 15 c3 f5 16 ef
♕×f5 17 ♗e2 e4 18 ♕b1 ef 19
♕×f5 ♖×f5 20 ♗×f3 ♖e5+
(U) when White is under heavy
pressure.

**C**

$\qquad$ **8 ♕d2** (20)

Compared with lines from the
previous chapter, White can now
play f3, relieving his king's bishop
from the task of guarding the
g-pawn, and he can also consider
♕g5 in some cases. But the
development of the queen's bishop
is impeded, so Black may get
equality by a slower plan than
usual.

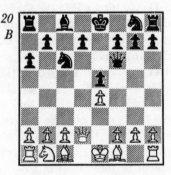

20
B

**8 ...** $\qquad$ **♕g6**

A critical line is 8 ... ♘ge7 9
♘c3 d6! e.g. 10 ♕g5 ♘b4 11
♗d3 ♗e6 12 ♕×f6 gf when:
a) **13 f4** d5 14 fe fe 15 ed ♘×d3+
16 cd ♘×d5 17 00 ♘×c3 18 bc
000∓ Buljovčić–Ciocaltea, Reggio
Emilia 1966–7.
b) **13 a3** ♘×d3+ 14 cd d5 15 00;
if Black plays ... d4, then followed
by f4, ♘e2 and ♘g3 may give
some chances to White – K.

$\qquad$ **9 ♘c3**

Better than 9 f3 d6 (9 ... ♘ge7
10 ♗d3 00 11 b3) 10 ♘a3 b5
11 ♗d3 (11 c4!? b4 12 ♘c2 –
Möhring) 11 ... ♘ge7 12 00 00

13 c3 f5∓ Möhring–Baumbach, E. German Ch 1963.

After 9 ♘c3:

C1 9 ... ♘ge7

C2 9 ... d5?!

**C1**

| 9 ... | ♘ge7 |
|---|---|
| 10 h4! | |

10 ♕g5 is premature, e.g. 10 ... d5 11 ♕×g6 hg 12 ♗d2 ♗e6 13 ed ♘×d5 14 ♘×d5 ♗×d5 15 000 000 16 f3 ♖d7 ½–½ Robatsch–Kottnauer, Beverwijk 1962. Not 10 b3 d5! – V.

| 10 ... | ♘d4 |
|---|---|

Others:

a) **10 ... b5** 11 h5 ♕g4:

a1) **12 ♕g5?** (Parma–de Rooi, Beverwijk 1964) 12 ... d5!, and not 12 ... ♕×g5.

a2) **12 f3!** ♕g3+ 13 ♔d1 – Parma.

b) **10 ... h5** 11 ♕g5! ♘b4 12 ♕×g6 ♘×g6 13 ♔d1 ♘e7 14 b3 f5 15 ♗a3 ♘bc6 (Bogdanović–Baumbach, E. Germany 1964) 16 ♗d3+ – B.

| 11 h5 | ♕c6 |
|---|---|
| 12 ♗d3 | |

Others:

a) **12 b3** when:

a1) **12 ... 00** 13 ♗a3 d6 14 f4 ♗e6 15 000 ♖fc8 16 ♔b2 f6 17 fe fe 18 ♗d3 h6 19 ♘d5± Bojković–Grigorian, Yugoslavia v USSR 1964.

a2) **12 ... d6!** e.g. 13 ♗a3 (13 f3 ♗e6 and 14 ... ♖c8) 13 ... ♗g4! 14 ♖c1 (14 f3? ♗×f3! or 14 ♗d3 ♖c8) 14 ... ♖c8 15 ♗b4

(or 15 ♗b2) 15 ... h6! followed by ... 00 with a good game for Black–Nunn and Povah.

b) **12 h6!?** g6 13 ♗d3 (Nunn) does not seem dangerous, as Black can play for an eventual ... f5 with greater effect than in the text (e.g. by ... d6, ... ♗e6, ... 000 etc.) since it is not so easy for White to organize a g-pawn break-through.

| 12 ... | h6 |
|---|---|
| 13 ♘e2 | ♘×e2 |
| 14 ♕×e2 | 00 |

15 ♗d2 d6 16 000 ♗e6 (16 ... f5!? is promising – V.) 17 ♔b1 and not now 17 ... ♕a4? (Nunn–Povah, Lambeth 1974) but 17 ... ♖fc8 (Povah) or possibly 17 ... ♖ac8 (Nunn). White's obvious plan is g4–g5, but Black has a sound position and the threat may not be too serious.

**C2**

| 9 ... | d5?!(21) |
|---|---|

Gipslis's suggestion, which is unsound.

21
W

| 10 ♘×d5! |
|---|

Others cannot test the idea:

a) **10 ♕×d5** (10 ed ♘d4) 10 ...
♘f6 11 ♕d6 ♗e6 12 f3 ♘d4 –
Gipslis.

b) **10 f3** ♘ge7 11 ed ♘d4 12 ♗d3
♗f5 13 ♗e4 ♖d8! 14 00 00:

b1) **15 ♕d3** ♘×d5 16 ♘×d5
♖×d5 17 ♗×f5 ♕×f5 ½–½
Klovan–Kapengut, USSR 1963.

b2) **15 ♕f2** b5 16 a3 ♗×d3 17 cd
f5 – CMQ.

| 10 ... | ♕×e4+ |
|---|---|
| 11 ♗e2 | ♕×g2 |
| 12 ♖f1 | ♖b8 |
| 13 ♘c7+ | ♔e7 |

CMQ gives this as unclear, but
our analysis shows that White is
winning due to the strength of his
queen's bishop on the a3–f8
diagonal:

14 b3!

The following variations show
that Black is defenceless:

a) **14 ... b5** 15 ♗a3+ b4 16
♘d5+ ♔e8 17 ♘×b4 ♘×b4
18 ♗×b4+.

b) **14 ... f6** 15 ♗a3+ ♔f7 16
♗c4+ ♔g6 17 000 threatening
18 ♖g1.

c) **14 ... ♕e4** (to pin the king's
bishop) 15 ♗a3+ ♔f6 16 ♘e8+
♔e6 (16 ... ♔f5 17 ♘d6+ or
16 ... ♔g6 17 ♖g1+) 17 ♕d6+
♔f5 18 ♕×b8! ♘×b8 19
♘d6+.

d) **14 ...** ♕×**h2** 15 ♗a3+ ♔f6
16 ♘e8+! ♔g6 17 000 and if 17
... ♕f4 18 ♖g1+ ♔h6 19 ♕×f4
ef 20 ♗f8 forces checkmate.

**D**

**8 ♕c7** (22)

This strange - looking move,
favoured by grandmaster Parma,
makes it hard for Black to achieve
his freeing advance ... d5 without
allowing exchanges that leave him
weak on the black squares in the
endgame.

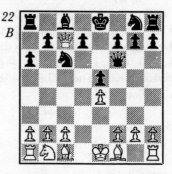

22
B

| 8 ... | ♘ge7 |
|---|---|

Others:

a) **8 ... d6** 9 ♘c3 ♕e7 10 ♘d5±
– G.

b) **8 ...** ♕**d8** 9 ♕×d8+ ♘×d8
10 ♘c3± since Black is two tempi
worse off than in A.

c) **8 ...** ♕**g6** 9 f3!? (9 ♘c3 ♘f6?
10 ♕d6± ; 9 ... ♘ge7 below)
9 ... ♘ge7 10 ♘c3 00 11 ♗e3 d6
(11 ... d5!? – G) 12 000 ♖d8
13 ♘d5± Vagdanash–Vereshnoi,
USSR 1956.

9 ♘c3

If 9 c4 ♕g6 10 f3 b5 (intending
... ♖b8–b7) 11 cb ab (Geissert–
Hennings, E. German Ch 1963)
is surely alright for Black?
Quieter play might allow White
to get a grip on d6, or other
Q-side weaknesses.

After 9 ♘c3:

D1 9 ... ♕e6!?

D2 9 ... 00

D3 9 ... ♘b4

Also:

a) **9 ...** ♕**g6** 10 ♗e3 00 11 000 b5 12 ♗c5 ♖e8 13 ♔b1 ♖b8 14 ♗×e7 ♖b7 (14 ... ♖×e7? 15 ♖d6 and 16 ♖×c6) 15 ♕d6 ♖×e7 16 ♕×g6 hg 17 ♘d5 ♖e6 18 g3! ♔f8 (18 ... ♘e7 19 ♗h3±) 19 h4! ♘e7 20 h5 g5 21 ♘e3±± Unzicker–Bazan, Buenos Aires 1960.

b) **9 ... b5!?** 10 ♗e3 00 (10 ... ♖b8!? 11 000!±):

b1) **11** ♗**c5** d6! 12 ♕×d6 ♕h4 13 g3? ♕h5 14 ♘d5 ♕f3! 15 ♘×e7+ ♘×e7 16 ♕×e7 ♗g4 17 ♖g1 ♖fd8 0–1 Peretjatkowicz–Bubenik, corres 1973–4.

b2) **11 000** ♘d4 (11 ... ♖b8) 12 g4?! (12 f4!± – Richter & Teschner, *Schach-Eroffnungen*) 12 ... b4 13 ♘a4 ♘ec6 14 ♗c4? (14 f4!) 14 ... ♖a7 15 g5 ♕e7 16 ♕b6 ♖b7! 17 ♕c5 (17 ♕×a6 ♖b8) 17 ... d6 18 ♕d5 ♗e6∓ Simek–Kupka, Prague 1963.

c) **9 ...** ♘**d4?!** 10 ♗d3 00 11 00 ♘g6 12 ♘d5 ♕c6 13 f4± Lambshire–Povah, Hammersmith 1972.

**D1**

    **9 ...**        ♕**e6!?** (*23*)

The main idea behind this move is to trap White's queen. The success of this plan in the game Bialas–Joppen (1961) was partly responsible for the 1960s

*23*
*W*

revival of the La Bourdonnais Variation.

D11 10 ♗d3

D12 10 ♗e3

D13 10 ♗g5!

10 b3!? remains untested:

a) **10 ... b5** 11 ♗b2 ♖a7 (11 ♖b8 12 000 ♘d4 13 f4) 12 ♕b6 00 13 000 d6 with chances for both sides – Harding and Pavah.

b) **10 ...** ♘**b4** (or 10 ... ♘d4) 11 ♗d3! e.g. 11 ... d5 12 ♗a3! – R, 1964.

c) **10 ... d5** 11 ed ♘×d5 12 ♘×d5 ♕×d5 13 ♗c4:

c1) **13 ...** ♕**d7** 14 ♕×d7+ ♗×d7 15 ♗a3.

c2) **13 ...** ♕**e4+** 14 ♗e3 00 15 00.

**D11**

    **10** ♗**d3**        **b5**

Or:

a) **10 ... d6** 11 ♗e3 00 – B.

b) **10 ... d5:**

b1) **11 00** 00 (11 ... d4 12 ♘e2) 12 f4± – R, 1963.

b2) **11** ♘**×d5** ♘×d5 12 ed ♕×d5 13 00± e.g. 13 ... 00 14 ♖e1 f5 15 b3 b5 16 c4! ♕d3 17

♕c6 ♗d7 18 ♕c5± – Matsukevich and Utyatsky.

11 ♗e3!

Not:

a) 11 00? ♖b8 12 f4 ♖b7 13 ♘d5 00 14 f5:

a1) 14 ... ♘×d5? 15 ♕×b7? (15 ♕×c8!) 15 ... ♕d6∓∓ Bialas – Joppen, W. German Ch 1961.

a2) 14 ... ♘×f5! 15 ef ♕×d5∓∓ – CMQ.

b) 11 f4 00 12 00 ♖b8 13 fe ♖b7 14 ♕d6 ♘×e5 Pietzsch–Zinn, E. German Ch 1962.

c) 11 ♕b6 ♘b4 12 ♕e3 d5 – G.

11 ...             00

Now if 11 ... ♖b8 12 ♗c5 ♖b7 13 ♕d6 – B.

| 12 ♗c5 | ♖e8 |
|---|---|
| 13 000 | ♔h8 |
| 14 ♗e2! | f5 |
| 15 ♗f3± | |

Cobo–From, Varna Olympiad 1962.

**D12**

| 10 ♗e3 | d5 |
|---|---|
| 11 ♗c5 | d4 |

11 ... 00!? 12 ed ♘×d5 13 ♘×d5 ♕×d5 is also quite promising for Black, in view of 14 ♗×f8? ♕e4+ 15 ♗e2? (15 ♔d2∓) 15 ... ♘d4 16 000 (16 00 ♗h3!) 16 ... ♘×e2+ 17 ♔b1 ♗f5 18 ♗c5? (better 18 f3 ♕a4 19 ♗a3 ♘d4) 18 ... ♕×c2+ 19 ♔a1 ♘d4 20 ♖c1? (20 ♖×d4 was the last chance.) 20 ... ♕b1+ 21 ♖×b1 ♘c2 mate; Postler–Arnold, Rukhla 1963.

12 000

Now:

a) 12 ... dc?? 13 ♖d6! ♕×a2 14 ♖d8+! ♘×d8 15 ♕e7 mate.

b) 12 ... b5!? 13 f4 and now:

b1) 13 ... b4? 14 ♘d5 ♘×d5 15 ed ♕×d5 16 ♗c4!± – G.

b2) 13 ... ♖b8? 14 ♗×e7! winning material, e.g. 14 ... ♖b7 15 ♘d5 G. Popov–Krstev, Bulgaria v. Yugoslavia corres 1964–5.

b3) 13 ... ♗d7! (CMQ) e.g. 14 f5!? ♕h6+ 15 ♔b1 ♖c8 16 ♕b7 ♖b8!?= – AHM.

c) 12 ... ♗d7:

c1) 13 ♕×b7? ♖b8 14 ♕c7 ♖c8 15 ♕b7 ♘d8 16 ♕a7 ♘ec6 and 17 ... dc – Müller.

c2) 13 ♘a4 b5 14 ♘b6 ♖a7 15 ♕d6 ♕×a2∓ – R. 1963,

c3) 13 f4 dc?! (13 ... b5 see b3) 14 ♗c4 ♖c8 15 ♕×b7 ♖b8 16 ♕×a6 with good attacking chances (16 ... ♗c8? 17 ♗×e6!) – G.

**D13**

10 ♗g5!

Ravinsky's refinement upon D12. If now 10 ... f6 11 ♗e3 and Black cannot play ... d5 because of the weakness of his g-pawn.

| 10 ... | d5 |
|---|---|
| 11 ♗×e7 | |

11 000?! d4 12 ♗c4? is refuted by 12 ... ♕×c4 13 ♗×e7 ♗e6! 14 ♘d5 (14 ♕×b7 ♖a7) 14 ... ♖c8 15 ♕×b7 ♘a5 – R, 1968.

| 11 ... | ♘×e7 |

12 000        d4
13 ♗c4±

a) **13 ...** ♕**h6+?** 14 ♔b1 00?
15 ♕ × e7 dc 16 ♕ × f7+! – G.

b) **13 ...** ♕**f6** 14 ♘d5 ♘ × d5 15
ed 00 16 ♖he1+ – U.

c) **13 ...** ♕**c6** 14 ♘d5 ♘ × d5
when:

c1) **15** ♕ × **e5+!?** ♘e7 16 ♕ × g7
♖f8 17 ♖ × d4 (17 ♕ × d4!? – B)
17 ... ♗e6 18 ♗d5!± –
Ravinsky.

c2) **15** ♕ × **c6+** bc 16 ed cd 17
♗ × d5 ♖a7 18 ♖he1± e.g. 18 ...
♖e7 19 c3 dc? 20 ♗c6+ – B.

**D2**

**9 ...**        **00**
10 ♗e3 (24)

Or 10 ♗d3:

a) **10 ... d5** 11 ed ♘d4 12 d6!
♘g6 13 d7 ♘h4 14 dc♕ ♘ × g2+
15 ♔f1 ♖a × c8 16 ♕ × b7 –
*Shakmaty v SSSR*, 1965.

b) **10 ...** ♘**b4** 11 00 ♘ec6 12 f4
b5 13 ♘d5 ♘ × d5 14 ed e4
15 dc ed ½–½ Ničevski–Kovačević,
Rovinj/Zagreb 1970.

c) **10 ...** ♕**g6** 11 00 d6 12 ♔h1
f5 is worth considering.

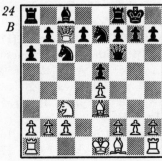

24
B

D21 10 ... d6
D22 10 ... d5?!

10 ... ♕g6, 10 ... b5!? see
above (p. 19).

**D21**

**10 ...**        **d6**
11 000        ♖d8
12 h4

Or:

a) **12** ♕**b6!?** threatening 13 ♘d5
– CMQ.

b) **12** ♗**c4** ♗g4 13 f3 ♖d7 14
♕b6 ♘c8 15 ♘d5 (Tan-de Rooi,
Amsterdam 1961) 15 ... ♕g6 16
♕b3 ♘a5 may equalize – Euwe.

12 ...        h6
13 ♘d5        ♘ × d5
14 ed        ♘d4
15 ♗ × d4        ed
16 ♕b6

a) **16 ...** ♗**f5** 17 ♕ × d4±
Mednis–Ennigrou, Varna Olympiad 1962.

b) **16 ...** ♕**f4+** (R, 1968) 17
♖d2 (17 ♔b1 ♖e8! with good
counter-chances) 17 ... ♖e8 18
♗d3± – U.

**D22**

**10 ...**        **d5?!**
11 ed

Not 11 ♘ × d5 ♘ × d5 12 ed
♘d4 13 ♗d3 ♗f5 14 ♗ × f5
♕ × f5 15 ♗ × d4 ed 16 00
♕ × d5 – *Shakhmaty v SSSR*.

11 ...        ♘d4

Or 11 ... ♘b4 12 000 ♗f5 13
♕b6 ♕ × b6 14 ♗ × b6 ♖ac8 15
d6± Tseshkovsky–Shtukaturkin,
Ordzhonikidze 1965.

12 000!

This is more precise than 12
♗d3 ♗f5 13 ♘e4? (13 000!? –
CMQ) 13 ... ♗×e4 14 ♗×e4
♘×d5! 15 ♗×d5 ♖ac8 16 ♕a5
♘×c2+ 17 ♔e2 ♘×e3 18 fe
♖c2+ 19 ♔d3 ♖8c8 20 ♖hf1
♕g6+ 21 ♗e4 ♕d6+ 22 ♕d5
♕b4 23 ♗×h7+ ♔h8 24 ♖fd1
e4+! 0–1 Ravinsky–Sutyeyev, ½-
final Burevestnik Ch, Moscow
1965.

> 12 ...              ♗f5
> 13 f4!              ♘×c2

Or 13 ... ♖ac8 14 fe ♕h4 15
g3! ♖×c7 16 gh ♘×c2 17 ♗b6
♖d7 18 a3± – R, 1968.

> 14 ♗c5             ♖fc8
> 15 ♕×e7            ♖×c5
> 16 ♕×c5            ♖c8

17 ♕×c8+! ♗×c8 18 ♔×c2
♕×f4 19 d6 ♗f5+ 20 ♗d3 e4
21 ♘×e4 ♗×e4 22 d7 ♕c7+
23 ♔b1 1–0 Parma–Ciocaltea,
Bucharest 1968.

**D3**

> 9 ...               ♘b4
> 10 ♗d3

Not 10 ♘a4?! b5! 11 ♘b6
(11 a3 ♕h4! – G) 11 ... ♘×c2+
12 ♔d1 ♘×a1 13 ♘×a8 00 14
♘b6 (14 ♗e3!?) 14 ... d5 with
a good game for Black – K.

> 10 ...              d5(*25*)
> 11 00

Others:

a) 11 ♘×d5 ♘e×d5 12 ed
♘×d3+! 13 cd 00 14 00 ♗f5
15 ♖e1 ♖fe8 16 ♗e3 ♗×d3 17
d6 ♗b5 18 d7 ♖ed8 19 ♖ad1
♗c6 20 ♖d6 ♕f5 with complica-

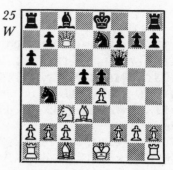

25
W

tions; Adams–Povah, Leeds 1973.

b) **11 ed!?** ♘e×d5 12 ♘×d5
♘×d5 13 ♕a5! (± – CMQ) is
worrying:

b1) **13 ...** ♗e6 14 ♗b5+ ♔f8
(14 ... ♔e7? 15 ♕a3+) is unattractive;

b2) **13 ...** ♕c6 14 c4 ♘e7 15
♕×e5 when:

b21) **15 ...** ♕×g2 16 ♗e4 ♕g4
17 f3 with a good ending ahead;

b22) **15 ... 00** 16 ♗e4 ♕×c4 17
b3± but not 17 ♕×e7? ♗g4! 18
f3 ♖fe8 19 ♕×b7 ♖ab8 20
♕a7 ♖×e4+ etc.

b3) **13 ...** ♘b6 14 ♗e3 ♘d7 15
♕a3 ♕e7 16 ♕×e7+ ♔×e7
17 000± – Harding and Povah.

b4) **13 ...** ♘e7 14 ♗b5+ ab!?
(14 ... ♘c6 15 ♗×c6 bc 16
♕c5±) 15 ♕×a8 ♕g6:

b41) **16 00?!** 00 17 ♗e3? (17
♕a3 ♘f5 with a good attack)
17 ... ♘d5! 18 ♕a3 (18 ♗c5?
♘f4 19 g3 ♘h3+ and 20 ...
♕c6+) 18 ... ♗h3 19 ♗g5
♘f4!∓ – V.

b42) **16 ♗e3!** is critical, e.g. 16
... 00 (16 ... ♕×g2 17 000) 17

♕a3 ♘c6 18 0-0-0 ♗f5 19 ♖d2 ♕×g2 20 ♖hd1 ♗g4 21 ♖e1 ♖c8 − V. This exchange sacrifice is possibly Black's best practical chance against 11 ed, but we do not think it can really be sound.

  11 ...                    d4

Not 11 ... 0-0?! 12 f4 ♘×d3 13 cd d4 14 ♘a4 ♗g4 15 ♘b6 ♖ad8 16 ♖f2± − Lemoine–Vyslouzil, Budapest 1959.

After the text move, White has a minimal advantage which in practice often peters out to a draw.

D31 12 ♘e2
D32 12 ♘a4!

**D31**

  **12 ♘e2**

D311 12 ... ♘×d3
D312 12 ... 0-0

**D311**

  **12 ...              ♘×d3**
  13 cd              ♘c6!

13 ... g5?! is risky, e.g. 14 ♗d2 ♘c6 15 ♖ac1 0-0 16 ♘g3 h6 17 b4 ♖e8 18 a4± Nezhmetdinov–Sakharov, Leningrad 1957.

  14 f4              ♕e7

  15 ♕×e7+

Or 15 ♕b6 ♕b4! 16 ♕×b4 ♘×b4 17 fe ♘×d3 18 ♘×d4 0-0= − CMQ.

  15 ...              ♔×e7
  16 fe              ♘×e5!?

Hoping for 17 ♘×d4 ♖d8=, but 16 ... ♗g4! is probably more awkward for White to meet. Two possibilities are:
a) **17 ♗g5+** ♔e8 18 ♘f4 ♘×e5

19 ♘d5 ♖c8 threatening ... ♗e2;
b) **17 ♘f4** ♘×e5 18 ♘d5+ ♔d6 19 b3 ♖ac8 20 ♗a3+ ♔e6 − Harding and Povah.

  17 b3!±

a) **17 ...** ♖**d8** 18 ♗a3+ ♔e8 19 ♘f4 f6 20 ♖ac1 ♘c6 21 ♗c5 Lukin–Ghizdavu, Leningrad v. Budapest students' match 1968.
b) **17 ... f6** 18 ♗a3+ ♔f7 19 ♖ac1 (19 ♘f4 is also good.) 19 ... ♖d8 20 ♖c7+ ♔g8 21 ♘f4 ♖d7 22 ♖fc1 (22 ♘d5!? ♘c6 23 ♖×f6!) 22 ... ♘c6 23 ♘d5 (1-0, 39) Kristoffel–Borodenko, corres 1971-3.

**D312**

  **12 ...              0-0**
  13 f4

13 ♗d2! is better;
a) **13 ... ♘ec6** 14 f4 ♗g4 15 fe ♕d8 16 ♕×d8 ♖a×d8 17 ♘f4 ♘×d3 18 cd ♘×e5 19 h3± − R, 1968.
b) **13 ... ♘×d3** 14 cd ♘c6 15 ♕b6! (15 f4 ♕d8!=) e.g. 15 ... ♕d8 16 ♕c5 ♗e6 17 f4± − U.

  13 ...              ♗g4!

This move was discovered by East German players during a training course. The old line was 13 ... ♘×d3 14 cd ♘c6 when 15 ♕b6 gives White a clear advantage, e.g. 15 ... ♕d8 16 ♕c5 ♕c7 17 ♗d2 ♗g4 18 ♘g3 ♗d7 19 ♖ac1 Kotov–Vladimirov, USSR 1959.

  14 fe

Not 14 ♘g3 ♖fc8 15 ♕×b7 ♖ab8 16 ♕a7 ♘ec6∓ − CMQ.

14 ...        ♕c6!
15 ♕×e7      ♘×d3
16 ♘×d4      ♕×e4

17 ♘f3 ♗×f3 18 cd ♕d4+ 19 ♖f2 ♗c6 20 ♕d6 ♖ad8 21 ♕×d4 ♖×d4 22 ♗d2 ½-½ Perfors–Baumbach, 5th Corres Olympiad 1962-4.

**D32**

12 ♘a4!(26)

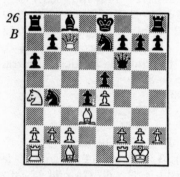

26
B

12 ...        ♕c6

12 ... ♘×d3 13 cd is inferior:
a) 13 ... 00 14 f4 see above, note to Black's 11th.
b) 13 ... ♕c6 14 ♕×c6+ ♘×c6 15 ♘b6 ♖b8 16 ♗d2 00 (Parma–Bleiman, Netanya 1971) 17 a4!± – Parma.

13 ♕×c6+

13 ♕a5 is innocuous, e.g. 13 ... ♘×d3 14 cd b5 15 ♘b6:
a) 15 ... ♕c7 16 ♗d2 ♖b8 17 ♘×c8 ♕×a5 18 ♘d6+ ♔d7 19 ♗×a5 ♔×d6 20 f4 ♘c6 21 fe+ ♔e6 22 ♗c7 ♖bc8 23 ♗b6 (23 ♗d6 f6) 23 ... ♖b8 24 ♗c5 ♖bd8= – B.
b) 15 ... ♖b8 16 ♘×c8 ♕×c8

17 f4 ♘c6 18 ♔e1 00 19 fe ♘×e5 20 ♕g3 f6 – R, 1968.

13 ...        ♘e×c6
14 ♘b6       ♖b8
15 f4!?

Surely White's main chances lie on the Q-side, in the advance of his b- and a-pawns? 15 ♗d2 comes into consideration, but Black is not forced to play ... ♘×d3, transposing to Parma-Bleiman. Instead 12 ...f6 or 12 ... ♗e6 give chances of equalizing.

15 ...        ♘×d3
16 cd         f6

Thus Black prevents the isolation of his queen's pawn, which had been fatal in D311. Boleslavsky comments: 'White stands better, but a clear way to realize this advantage is not to be found'. For example, if White tries 17 f5 (intending ♗d2, ♖fc1, b4, a4 etc.), Black can play 17 ... ♗d7 followed by the manoeuvre ... ♘e7–c8, after which he can even think about a counter-attack by ... ♖g8, ... g6 etc. – K. Further investigation of these confusingly similar lines is necessary before firm conclusions can be drawn.

**E**

8 ♕a3(27)

The evident intention of this move is to hinder Black's castling, by controlling the weakened a3-f8 diagonal. The move was first played by Spassky, and has been quite popular ever since; but it is

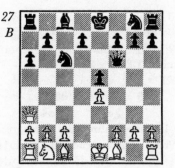

27
B

not dangerous to Black with best play.

E1 8 ... ♕g6

E2 8 ... ♘ge7!

8 ... ♘d4?! 9 ♗d3 ♕g6 10 00:

a) **10 ... ♘f3+** 11 ♔h1 ♕h5 (11 ... ♘h4 12 g3) 12 h3 d5 13 ♗e2 de 14 ♕a4+ ! – G.

b) **10 ... d5** 11 ed ♗f5 (11 ... ♘f3+ 12 ♔h1 ♕h5 13 ♗b5+ – U) 12 ♗×f5 ♕×f5 13 ♘c3 000 14 ♗e3 ♔b8 15 ♕c5 ♘f6 16 f4 ♘e4 17 ♕b6 ♖d6? 18 fe!± Sakharov–Kapengut, USSR 1963.

**E1**

**8 ...    ♕g6**

Practically forcing White to gambit a pawn.

9 ♗e3!

Not 9 ♘c3? ♘d4! 10 ♕a4 (10 ♗d3 ♕×g2) 10 ... ♖b8 threatening ... b5∓ – U.

9 ...        ♕ × e4

10 ♘c3       ♕b4

Neither 10 ... ♕×c2? 11 ♘d5! nor 10 ... ♕g6 11 ♘b5! are viable.

11 ♕ × b4     ♘ × b4

12 000       ♘e7

Others:

a) **12 ... b5** 13 ♗c5 ♘c6 14 ♘e4± Honfi–Barcza, Novi Sad 1962.

b) **12 ...♘f6** 13 ♗c5! ♘c6 14 f4 d6 (14 ... ef? 15 ♖e1+ ♔d8 16 ♗b6 mate) 15 ♗×d6 ef 16 ♗c4 ♗e6 17 ♖he1 ♘d8 18 ♗b3 ♖c8 19 ♘a4± Cheremisin–Ivlev, ½-final Moscow Ch 1962.

13 ♗c5       ♘bc6

14 ♗c4!?

Also good:

a) **14 f4** d5 (14 ... ef 15 ♗c4 00 16 ♖he1 – B) 15 fe ♗e6 16 ♗d6 d4 (16 ... 00 17 ♗e2 ♖fe8 18 ♗f3 d4 19 ♘a4 – U) 17 ♘e4 ♗d5 18 ♗d3 ♘c6 19 c4! dc 20 ♘×c3 ♗e6 21 ♖he1± Spassky–Utyatsky, Kislovodsk 1960.

b) **14 ♘e4** d5 15 ♘d6+ ♔d7 16 ♘×f7 ♖f8 17 ♘g5± Tal–Grave, Latvian Ch 1965.

14 ...        b5

15 ♘d5

Or 15 ♗d5 ♖b8 16 ♘e4 ♘×d5 17 ♘d6+ ♔e7 18 ♖×d5 ♔e6 19 ♖hd1± Kanko–Simonen, Finland 1963.

15 ...        ♘ × d5

15 ... bc is weaker, e.g. 16 ♘c7+ ♔d8 17 ♘×a8 d5 18 ♘b6 ♗e6 19 ♗×e7+ ♘×e7 20 ♘×c4±± Zhidkov – Mnatsakanian, Leningrad 1964.

16 ♗ × d5     ♗b7?

Or 16 ... f6 17 f4 ♗b7 18 fe fe 19 ♖hf1 000 20 ♖f7 with good play for the pawn – Matanović, *Informator* 5.

17 ♗×f7+! ♔d8
18 ♖he1 ♔c8
19 f3 ♘d8
20 ♗h5 ♘e6 21 ♖×e5 ♘×c5
22 ♖×c5+ ♔d8 23 ♗g4 ♗c8
24 h4 ♖e8 25 ♖×c8+! 1–0
Stankov–Bashev, Bulgaria 1968.

**E2**

**8 ...                ♘ge7!**

9 ♘c3 (28)

Not 9 ♗e3? d5:

a) **10 ♗c5** ♘d4 11 ♗×e7? ♕f4!
12 ♔d1 ♕×f2 13 ♗d3 de 14
♖f1 ♗g4+ 15 ♔c1 ♕e3+ 16
♘d2 ed 17 ♗c5 ♖c8 18 ♕a4+
b5 19 ♗×d4 ed 0–1 Kliner–
Soltis, Czech Corres Ch 1973.

b) **10 ed** ♘×d5 11 ♗c5 ♕g6
12 ♕d3 (12 ♕b3 ♕e4+ 13 ♗e2
♘f4) 12 ... ♕×d3 13 ♗×d3
♘db4 14 ♔d2 ♘×d3 15 ♔×d3
♗f5+ 16 ♔d2 f6∓ – V.

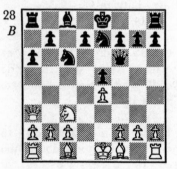

28
B

E21 9 ... 00
E22 9 ... ♘d4
E23 9 ... ♖b8!

9 ... ♕g6 10 ♗e3 d5 11 ed
♘d4 12 ♗×d4 ed 13 ♕a4+ ♗d7
14 ♕×d4 ♕×c2 15 ♗d3 ♕×b2
16 ♖b1 ♕a3 17 ♖×b7 ♖c8

18 ♖b3 ♕c1+ 19 ♘d1 ♕g5
20 d6 ♘c6 21 ♕a4+ ♔f8
22 00± Mnatsakanian–Monti,
Budva 1963.

**E21**

**9 ...                00**

10 ♗e3 ♘d4
Drimer–Baumbach, Bucharest
1962, went instead 10 ... d5!?
11 ♘×d5 ♘×d5 12 ed ♘d4
13 ♗d3 ♗f5 14 ♗×d4 ed 15 000
♖ac8 16 ♕b3±.

11 000

11 ♗d3 comes into consideration.

11 ...              d6
12 ♗c4            ♗d7
13 ♔b1            ♗c6

14 ♘e2 ♘×e2 15 ♖×d6 ♕h4
16 ♗×e2 ♗×e4 17 f3 ♗c6±
Seuss–Avner, Student Olympiad,
Krakow, 1964.

**E22**

**9 ...                ♘d4**

Suggested by Ilivitsky.

10 ♗d3            ♖b8
Probably better:

a) **10 ... 00** 11 ♗e3 (11 h4!? – G)
11 ... d6 12 000 ♖b8 13 h4 b5
14 b4 ♗b7 15 f3 ♖fc8 16 ♔d2
♖c7 17 ♖c1 ♖ac8 18 ♘d1 d5∓
Pogats–Szily, Kecskemet 1962.

b) **10 ... ♕g6** e.g.:

b1) **11 00** ♘f3+ 12 ♔h1 ♕h5
13 h3 d6 14 ♗e2 ♗×h3 15 ♗×f3
♗g4+ 16 ♔g1 ♗×f3 17 gf
♕g6+ 18 ♔h2 ♕h5+ ½–½
Burlyaev–Matsukevich, Moscow
1963.

b2) **11 ♗e3!?** ♖b8 (11 ... ♕×g2

12 000 with good play – B) 12
♕c5 d6 13 ♕c7 ♘ec6 14 ♘d5 00
with a complicated position (½–½,
54); Mednis–Martz, USA Ch
1973.

Can White find something more
convincing in these lines?

    11 ♘e2

Or:

a) **11 00** b5 12 ♘d5 ♘ × d5 13 ed
b4 14 ♕a5 00∓ and not now 15
f4? e4! 16 ♗ × e4 ♘e2+ 17 ♔h1
♕h4 18 ♗d3 ♘g3+∓∓ Zak-
harov–Strekalovsky, USSR Spartakiad 1963.

b) **11 ♗e3!?** b5 12 ♗ × d4 ed
13 ♘e2 00 14 ♕c5 ♘c6 15 f4!
♖e8 16 00± (1–0, 30) Schutt–
Braunstein, ½-final 6th Corres
Olympiad 1966–7.

    11 ...        ♘ × e2
    12 ♗ × e2    00
    13 ♗e3       b5

14 ♗c5 ♖e8 15 000 ♘g6 16 g3
♕c6 17 f3 ♗b7 18 ♖d6±
Selivanovsky    –    Matsukevich,
Harkov 1963.

**E23**

    9 ...        ♖b8!*(29)*

29
W

    10 ♗e3

    10 ♘d5!? (10 h4?! b5! – V)
10 ... ♘ × d5 11 ed is also
interesting:

a) **11 ... ♘d4!?** 12 ♗d3 b5 13 00
♗b7 14 ♗e3 with complications
– K;

b) **11 ... ♘e7** when:

b1) **12 c4** b5 13 h4 ♕g6= Szily–
Baumbach, Bad Liebenstein 1963,
went om 14 ♖h3? bc 15 ♖e3
16 ♗ × c4 ♕g4 17 ♕c3 ♘f5
18 ♗e2 ♕ × h4 19 ♖h3 ♕e4 and
Black won.

b2) **12 ♗e3!** is critical:

b21) **12 ... ♘ × d5?** 13 ♗a7 ♖a8
14 ♗c5 with good play for the
pawn – K;

b22) **12 ... d6!?** 13 000 00 (13 ...
♗f5 14 ♕a4+) 14 ♗d3 or 14
♗b6± – V.

b23) **12 ... b5!** see E231.

    10 ...        b5
    11 ♘d5       ♘ × d5
    12 ed

E231 12 ... b4!
E232 12 ... ♘e7
E231

    **12 ...**        **b4!**
    13 ♕d3

a) **13 ♕a4** (Honfi–Baumbach,
corres 1963–5) 13 ... ♘d4 14 000
00 and White had difficulty in
co-ordinating his pieces – B.

b) **13 ♕b3** when:

b1) **13 ... ♘e7** 14 ♗a7 (or 14 000
00= Neikirch–Baumbach, E.
German Team Ch 1964) 14 ...
♖b7 15 ♗c5 d6 16 ♗ × a6 dc 17
♗ × b7 ♗ × b7 18 ♕a4+ ♔d8 19

♕a5+ ♔d7 20 ♕b5+ ♔c8 21
♕×c5+ ♔b8 22 ♖d1 ♖d8 23
d6 ♘f5 24 ♕c7+ ½-½ Link–
Baumbach, corres 1962–4.

b2) **13 ... ♘d4!?** 14 ♗×d4 ed
15 000 00= – Matsukevich and
Utyatsky.

13 ...          ♘e7

According to Baumbach, Black
has no satisfactory defensive line
now. On the contrary, imagina-
tive play gives him good attacking
chances!

14 d6!?

Others:

a) **14 ♕d2** when:

a1) **14 ... ♕d6** 15 000 ♗b7 16
f4± Zuidema–de Rooi, Beverwijk
1964.

a2) **14 ... 00** 15 ♗c4 (15 000 d6
is critical.) 15 ... ♕d6! 16 00
♘f5!= P. N. Lee–Povah, Leeds
1971.

a3) **14 ... ♘f5** 15 ♗a7? (15 000;
15 ♗d3) 15 ... ♖b7 16 ♗c5 a5
17 a3 d6∓ Coleman–Povah,
Enfield 1975.

b) **14 000** 00 (14 ... ♗b7!?)
15 h4:

b1) **15 ... ♘f5** 16 ♗g5 ♕g6 17
g4 ♘d4 18 ♗e7 ♖e8 19 ♕×g6
hg 20 ♗d6± Gurvich–Baumbach,
Ukraine v. E. Germany corres
1963–5.

b2) **15 ... ♕d6!** with ideas of ...
♖b5 followed by ... ♗b7, and
possibly ... f5 if White omits g4
– V.

14 ...          ♘f5
15 000          ♗b7

16 ♗c5

Or 16 ♖g1 00:

a) **17 ♗e2** a5 (possibly better 17
... ♖fc8 – V) 18 ♗g4 (Stean–
Povah, Charlton 1975) 18 ...
♘×e3∓ – Stean.

b) **17 g4** ♘h4! 18 g5 ♕e6 19
♔b1 (19 ♔b3 a5∓) 19 ... e4
20 ♕b3 a5 21 ♕×e6 fe∓
Hershman–Povah, British Junior
Ch 1971.

16 ...          00
17 ♗×b4        ♗×g2
18 ♗×g2        ♖×b4
19 ♗e4

a) **19 ... ♖d4?** 20 ♕f3 ♕h6+
(20 ... ♘×d6 21 ♕×f6 gf 22
♖×d4+) 21 ♔b1 ♘×d6 (21 ...
♘h4!?) 22 ♖×d4 ed 23 ♗d3±
Fichtl–Smejkal, Prague 1963. In
view of this game, Baumbach and
others considered the position
after White's 19th to be ±, but
Black has two better moves
available:

b) **19 ... ♘h4!** (Stean) e.g. 20
♗d5 (20 ♗×h7+ ♔h8 threatening ... ♕h6+ or 20 ♔b1 ♖fb8
21 b3 ♖d4 22 ♕e2 ♖×d6) 20
... ♖fb8 (20 ... e4 21 ♕c3) 21
♗b3 a5 22 a4 ♘f3 with good
attacking chances for Black – V.

c) or even **19 ... ♖fb8!?** e.g.
20 ♗×f5 (20 b3 ♕h6+ 21 ♔b1
♖d4 22 ♕f3 ♘×d6) 20 ... e4
21 ♗×e4? (21 ♕c3 ♕×f5∓)
21 ... ♕×b2+ 22 ♔d2 ♖d4
winning White's queen, or 21
♗×h7+ ♔×h7 22 ♕h3+ ♔g8
with a big attack for Black – V.

**E232**

    **12 ...**         ♘e7 *(30)*

E2321 13 000
E2322 13 ♗c5!?

**E2321**

    **13 000**       d6

   Others:

a) **13 ... ♘f5** = (14 ♗c5 d6) – B.
b) **13 ... ♗b7** 14 f4! (14 d6!?)
14 ... ♘ × d5 (14 ... ef 15 ♗d4!)
15 fe ♕c6 (15 ... ♕ × e5 16 ♗d2)
16 ♗d2 ♕b6 17 e6! fe 18 ♕g3 00
19 ♗h6 g6 20 ♕e5 ♘f6 21
♖ × d7! ♗e4 22 ♗d3! ♗ × d3
23 ♖ × d3 ♖f7 24 ♖hd1 (±)
24 ... ♘g4? 25 ♕ × b8+ ! 1–0
Bönsch–Flechsig, Jena 1967.

    **14 h4!**       h6
    **15 ♗e2**     ♗b7

15 ... ♘f5 is slightly stronger.
Honfi – Damjanović, Reggio
Emilia 1966–7, continued 16 g4!
(± – U) 16 ... b4!? 17 ♕a4+
♗d7 18 ♕ × a6 ♘ × e3 19 fe 00
with some chances for the pawn
(½–½, 37 after inaccuracies by
White).

    **16 ♗f3**      00
    **17 ♗e4**     b4

    18 ♕d3      ♗c8
19 f3 ♗f5 20 g4± Honfi–Pietszch,
Kecskemet 1962.

**E2322**

    **13 ♗c5!?**     ♘ × d5
    **14 000**      ♗b7 *(31)*

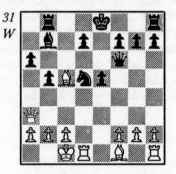

    15 ♗ × b5!?

White gets nowhere with:
a) **15 ♗d3** b4! 16 ♗ × b4 ♘ × b4
17 ♕ × b4 ♕e7 18 ♕g4 00 19
♖he1 d5 20 ♕h5 e4 Bokuchava–
Grigorian, Kishinev 1964.
b) **15 ♗d6** b4 16 ♗ × b4 ♘ × b4
17 ♕ × b4 ♕e7 18 ♕d6 ♖c8! –
K.

    **15 ...**      ab
    **16 ♕a7**     ♕d8
    **17 ♗d6**     ♘c7
    **18 ♖he1**    f6

A complicated position, but we
believe Black is all right.

    19 f4

Or 19 ♖d3 ♘a6 20 ♖ed1 ♗c6
21 f4 e4∓ Klompus–Silverberg,
7th USSR Corres Ch 1964–5.

    **19 ...**      e4
    **20 ♖e3?!**

White might keep balanced

chances by 20 ♕b6 ♗c6 21 ♕×c7 ♕×c7 22 ♗×c7 as in Popov–Silverberg, Bulgaria v. Ukraine corres, 1964–5.

20 ...  ♔f7!

Improving upon 20 ... ♔c8? of Kupreichik–Ghizdavu, Riga 1967; White could then play 21 ♕b6 ♘e6? (20 ... ♗c6± with a tempo down on the previous note) 22 f5 ♘g5 23 h4 ♘f7 24 ♗×b8 ♕×b8 25 ♖×e4+ ♘e5 26 ♕×b5 (threatening 27 ♖b4±±) – B.

21 ♖b3

Not 21 ♕b6? (or 21 ♖c3?) 21 ... ♘d5 attacking the rook.

21 ...  ♖e8

Or 21 ... ♕c8 22 ♕b6 ♗d5.

22 ♕b6  ♗d5!∓

a) 23 ♕×c7 ♕×c7 24 ♗×c7 ♗×b3 25 ♗×b8 ♖×b8 26 ab ♔e6∓.

b) 23 ♗×c7 ♖×b6 24 ♗×d8 ♗×b3 25 ♗×b6 ♗e6∓ – AHM.

Conclusion

8 ♕×f6 and 8 ♕d3 are innocuous, and 8 ♕d2 (though commanding more respect) should also permit comfortable equality. 8 ♕a3, once thought strong, gives Black good chances thanks to our improvements in the Fichtl–Smejkal line (p. 28) and in E2322. However, Black needs something more convincing against 8 ♕c7, as, after 8 ... ♘ge7 9 ♘c3 ♘b4 10 ♗d3 d5, White can play for somewhat favourable endings in D31 and D32, while the untested Baumbach suggestion 11 ed (note b to White's eleventh move, p. 22) may even be a refutation of the usual ways of handling 8 ♕c7.

# 3 4 ... e5, Unusual Lines

In the previous two chapters, we have seen the main battle-lines of the La Bourdonnais Variation drawn up around the 'hunt variation'. Prior to the 1950s, however, this was not the most common way to handle the position after 1 e4 c5 2 ♘f3 ♘c6 3 d4 cd 4 ♘×d4 e5. In this chapter we look at the older methods, which are still employed from time to time.

     1 e4            c5
     2 ♘f3       ♘c6

2 ... d6 3 d4 cd 4 ♘×d4 e5!? is illogical because after 5 ♗b5+ ♗d7 6 ♗×d7+ ♕×d7 7 ♘f3 ♘f6 8 ♘c3 we have a Boleslavsky or Najdorf type of position in which Black has exchanged his better bishop for White's inferior one. Kapengut–Ustinov, 6th USSR Spartakiad 1975, continued 8 ... h6 9 00 ♘a6 10 ♕e2 ♘c7 11 ♖d1 ♕c6 12 a4 ♗e7 13 ♖d3 a6 14 a5 ♘b5 15 ♘d5 ♘×d5 16 ed ♕d7 17 c4 ♘a7 18 ♘e1 00 19 ♕h5 ♖fc8 20 b3 ♗f8 21 ♖g3 ♔h7 22 ♘f3 ♖c7 23 ♘g5+ ♔h8 24 ♘e4 (threatening 25

♗×h6 gh 26 ♘f6 and 27 ♖g8 mate) 24 ... ♗e7 (24 ... f5 also allows the combination.) 25 ♗×h6 g6 26 ♘g5! ♗f6 27 ♕f3 ♕f5 28 ♘e4 (1–0, 42).

     3 d4            cd
     4 ♘×d4     e5 (32)

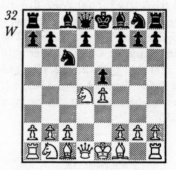

A 5 ♘×c6
B 5 ♘f5
C 5 ♘e2
D 5 ♘b3
E 5 ♘f3
F 5 ♘b5!

## A

     5 ♘×c6

This move, the first to be tried by 19th Century experts, gives the game a very different character from the 'hunt variation'.

Instead of the black square holes, Black gets the b-file for his rook and a mobile central pawn majority. White cannot do anything with the time saved by exchanging knights, and as players became conscious of this so the move went out of fashion.

5 ...          bc
6 ♗c4

Or 6 c4 ♘f6 7 ♗g5 ♕a5+ or 7 ♘c3 ♗b4 – V.

6 ...          ♘f6

Or:

a) **6 ... ♗a6!?** 7 ♗×a6? (7 ♕d3= – G) 7 ... ♕a5+ – Löwenthal.

b) **6 ... ♗c5** 7 00 ♘e7 8 ♕h5 ♘g6 9 ♘c3 d6 10 ♘e2 (10 ♘a4 – Linder, in 'A. D. Petroff–The First Russian Chess Master') 10 ... 00 11 ♗b3 a5 12 c3 ♗a6 13 ♖e1 ♕b6 14 ♕f3 (1–0, 67) Petroff–Shumov, St Petersburg 1853.

7 ♗g5

Others:

a) **7 ♘c3** see page 38.

b) **7 00** when:

b1) **7 ... ♘×e4?** 8 ♖e1 d5? 9 ♖×e4! – U.

b2) **7...d5?!** Morphy–Löwenthal (page x).

b3) **7 ... ♗e7** (*Handbuch*) 8 ♘c3 d6 and 9 ... 00= – Euwe.

c) **7 ♕e2** ♗e7 8 ♘c3 00 9 ♗g5 ♘×e4! 10 ♗×e7 ♘×c3 11 ♕×e5! ♖e8 12 00 ♕×e7 13 ♕×c3 d5 (½–½, 29) MacDonnell–La Bourdonnais, 1835.

7 ...          ♗e7

Another MacDonnell – La Bourdonnais game went 7 ... ♗c5!? 8 00 h6 9 ♗×f6 ♕×f6 10 ♘c3 a5 11 ♔h1 d6 12 ♕d2 g5 13 ♖ad1 ♔e7 14 ♘a4 ♗d4 15 ♕d3 h5 with a complicated position (½–½, 56).

8 ♕e2

Chigorin preferred 8 ♘c3 ♗b7 9 ♕e2 d5 10 ♖ad1, but 10 ... d4 might be good then.

8 ...          d5

8 ... 00 might be better; not then 9 ♘c3 (note c to White's 7th).

9 ♗×f6!?

Neishtadt prefers 9 ed cd 10 ♗b5+ ♗d7 11 ♗×d7+ ♘×d7 12 ♗×e7 ♕×e7 13 ♘c3.

The text move was played in the most famous La Bourdonnais game, perhaps, of his whole career – complete in the introduction (p. x).

**B**

5 ♘f5          d5!
6 ♕×d5

If 6 ♘g3, Black does not have to play as badly as in the 1937 game Krstens–Frizike: 6 ... d4 (or 6 ... de 7 ♕×d8+ ♔×d8=) 7 f4 ♗d6 8 f5 ♘f6 9 a3 ♕c7 10 ♗d3 ♗d7 11 00 00? 12 ♘d2 ♖ac8 13 ♘h5 ♘×h5? (13 ... ♗e7) 14 ♕×h5 ♔h8? (14 ... ♗e7; not 14 ... f6 15 ♗c4+ ♔h8 16 ♖f3) 15 f6 g6 16 ♕h6 ♖g8 17 ♘f3 ♗f8 18 ♘g5! 1–0.

6 ...          ♕×d5

7 ed      ♗×f5
8 dc      bc
9 c3 ♖b8 10 ♘d2 ♗c5 11 ♘b3
♗b6 12 ♗c4 ♘e7 13 00 00=
– U.

## C

5 ♘e2      ♘f6
6 ♘ec3
For 6 ♘bc3 see page 40.
6 ...      ♗c5
7 ♗c4      d6
8 a3?      ♘g4∓
9 ♗e3 (9 00? ♕h4) 9 ... ♘×e3
10 fe ♕g5 (10 ... ♗×e3? 11
♕f3) 11 ♕f3 ♕×e3+ 12 ♕×e3
♗×e3 13 ♘d5 ♗b6 (0–1, 46)
Weenink–Sultan Khan, Hamburg
1930.

## D

5 ♘b3 *(33)*
Suggested by Staunton in *The
Chess Player's Handbook*!

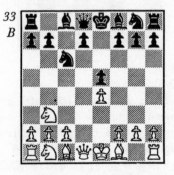

5 ...      ♗b4+!?
5 ... ♘f6 is simpler:
a) **6 ♗c4** (6 ♘c3 page 39) 6 ... d6
(6 ... ♗b4+!?) 7 ♘c3 (also like
Lasker's Variation) 7 ... ♗e6 8
♗d5 ♗e7 9 00 00 10 ♗e3 ♕d7
11 ♕d2 ♘b4 12 c3 ♖fc8 13 a3

♘b×d5 14 ed ♗f5 15 ♖ac1 ♗g6
16 ♕e2 ♘e8 17 g4?! f5 18 ♘d2
♘f6 (0–1, 49) Golmayo–Sultan
Khan, Hamburg 1930.
b) **6 ♗g5** ♗b4+ 7 c3 ♗e7 8
♗×f6 ♗×f6 9 ♘c4 00 10 ♕d3
d6 11 ♘1d2 ♗e7 12 00 ♔h8 13
♖ad1 f5 (13 ... ♗e6!?) 14 ♗d5
♕c7? (14 ... f4 15 f3 ♕e8 is
much better.) 15 ♘c4 ♖f6 16
♘3d2 f4 17 f3 ♗d7 18 b4±
Maté-Turi, Hungarian Corres Ch
1964–5.

6 c3
Better 6 ♗d2 – G, e.g. 6 ... ♗e7
7 ♘c3 ♘f6 8 ♗g5 (compare
chapter 5, A).
6 ...      ♗e7
7 ♗c4
Or 7 c4 ♘f6 8 ♗d3 00 9 00 d6
10 ♘c3 ♗e6 11 ♗g5 h6 12
♗×f6 ♗×f6 13 ♘d5 ♗×d5 14
ed ♘d4= Mukhin–Burlyaev,
Tashkent 1963.
7 ...      ♘f6
8 ♕d3      00
9 00      d6
10 ♘a3 ♗e6 11 ♖d1 a6 12 ♗g5
♘e8 13 ♗×e7 ♘×e7 14 ♗×e6
fe 15 ♘c4 ♘g6! when the
weakness of Black's d-pawn is
balanced by the activity of his
pieces, e.g. 16 ♘×d6?? ♘f4 17
♕d2 ♕g5∓∓ Bannik –
Kuzminikh, Leningrad ½-final
15th USSR Ch 1946.

## E

5 ♘f3
According to G, this move was
played in a Staunton–St. Amant

encounter, but Coles and Keene (authors of *Howard Staunton*) have not been able to trace any such game – it was certainly not in the Paris match of 1843. Perhaps the Yugoslavs were misled by their sources? Coles points out that two Cochrane–Staunton games of the same vintage got into this line by 1 e4 c5 2 d4 cd 3 ♕×d4?! ♘c6 4 ♕d1 e5?! 5 ♗c4 ♘f6 6 ♘c3 – see Staunton's Handbook, p. 389! [This would appear to stem from a similar reference in Bilguer's *Handbuch*, probably based on the eighth and tenth games of the 1843 match which opened 1 e4 c5 2 ♘f3 e6 3 d4 cd 4 ♘×d4 ♘c6 5 ♘f3, or, perhaps, on a misunderstanding of p. 371 of *The Chess Player's Handbook* (2nd edition). – Editor.]

5 ...          ♘f6

Or:

a) **5 ...** ♗**e7** transposing to the Lasker Variation (p. 40) after 6 ♘c3 ♘f6.

b) **5 ...** ♗**c5** 6 ♗c4 d6 'comes into consideration' – G.

6 ♗c4

Others:

a) **6** ♗**g5** ♗c5 (6 ... ♗e7 7 ♘c3 ♘f6 Lasker Var.) 7 ♗×f6 gf (Better 7 ... ♕×f6 – Euwe) 8 ♗c4± Euwe – Chepurnov, Amateur World Ch, The Hague 1928.

b) **6** ♗**d3** ♗c5 (= Staunton) 7 00 d6 when both 8 h3 h6 and 8 h3 h6 and 8 ♗g5 ♗g4 were

tried in Cochrane – Staunton games.

6 ...          ♗c5

Not 6 ... ♘×e4? 7 ♗×f7+ ♔×f7 8 ♕d5+.

| 7 | 00 | 00 |
| 8 | ♘c3 | h6 |
| 9 | a3 | a6 |
| 10 | ♗d5 | d6 |

Cochrane – Staunton, London 1843; (0–1, 26) loc. cit. Apparently this line was quite common in London at that time.

**F**

5 ♘**b5!** (*34*)

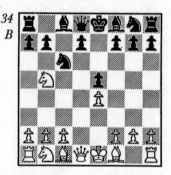

34
B

F1 5 ... d6
F2 5 ... a6

a) **5 ...** ♗**c5** 6 ♘1c3 ♘f6 see page 42.

b) **5 ...** ♘**f6** 6 ♗g5 (6 ♘1c3 page 42) 6 ... ♗c5 (6 ... d6 7 ♗×f6 gf 8 ♗c4±) 7 ♘d6+ ♔e7 (7 ... ♔f8 8 ♗c4±±) 8 ♘f5+ ♔f8 9 ♘c3 d6 10 ♘e3 h6 11 ♗×f6 ♕×f6 12 ♘cd5± – U.

c) **5 ... h6** 6 ♘d6+ (6 ♘1c3 ♘f6 page 42) 6 ... ♗×d6 7 ♕×d6 ♕e7 8 ♕×e7+ ♗g×e7 9 ♘c3 ♘b4 10 ♗d3 d5 11 ed ♘×d3+

12 cd ♗f5 13 d6 ♘c6 14 ♗e3
♗×d3 15 000± – U.

**F1**

   **5 ...        d6**
   6 ♘1c3

Or:

a) **6 c4 ♗e7** 7 ♘1c3 a6 8 ♘a3
♘f6 9 ♗e2 00 10 ♗e3 ♗e6 11 00
♖c7 12 ♖c1 h6 13 ♕d2 ♘e8±
Suetin–Kopayev, USSR 1952.

b) **6 ♗c4!?** when:

b1) **6 ... ♗e6** 7 ♘1a3 (7 ♗d2!?)
7 ... a6 8 ♘c3 ♘f6 9 ♗e3?! (9
♗g5! like Lasker's Variation)
9 ... b5 10 ♗d5 ♖c8 11 ♘e2 b4
12 ♘c4 ♗×d5 13 ed ♘e7 14
♗b6 ♕d7 15 b3 ♘e×d5 16 a3?
♖×c4 17 bc ♘×b6 (0–1, 44)
Apscheneek – Sultan Khan,
Hamburg 1930.

b2) **6 ... a6** 7 ♘5c3 f5?! (but
7 ... ♘f6 8 ♗g5 or 7 ... ♗e6 8
♘d5) 8 ef ♗×f5 9 ♗d3 ♗×d3
10 ♕×d3 ♘b4 11 ♕e2 ♘f6 12
00 ♗e7 13 f4± Averbakh–
Kuzminikh, Leningrad ½-final
15th USSR Ch 1946.

   6 ...        a6
6 ... ♘f6 see p. 45 (Lasker
Variation again).

   7 ♘a3        h6

Others:

a) **7 ... ♘f6** Lasker Var.

b) **7 ... ♗e6** 8 ♘c4 ♖c8 9 ♘d5
♗×d5 10 ed ♘b8 11 ♗e2 ♘d7
12 00 ♘gf6 13 a4 ♗e7 14 ♗e3 00
15 a5!± Matanović–Larsen,
Beverwijk 1960.

c) Kuzminikh suggested **7 ... b5!?**
in his 1951 survey of the La

Bourdonnais Variation; Lokvenc–
Padevsky, Debrecen 1961, continued 8 ♘d5 ♘f6 9 ♗e3 ♘×d5
10 ♕×d5 ♕c7 11 c4 ♗e6 12
♕d3 b4 13 ♘c2 ♗e7=.

   8 ♘c4

Or 8 ♘d5 ♘f6 9 ♘×f6+
♕×f6 10 ♘c4 ♕h4 11 ♗d3
♗g4 12 ♕d2 ♗e7 13 00 00 14
♘b6 (1–0, 37) Karasev–Klaman,
Kronshtadt 1975.

   8 ...        b5
   9 ♘e3        ♘f6
   10 ♘ed5        ♗e7
11 ♗e3 00 (11 ... ♖b8!? – U)
12 a4 b4 13 ♗b6 ♕d7 14
♘×f6+ ♗×f6 15 ♘d5 with a
very promising position for White;
Aronin–Kuzminikh, ½-final 16th
USSR Ch 1948.

**F2**

   **5 ...        a6**

This is the usual move. It is
not merely provocative, for at a6
the pawn serves to keep white
pieces out of b5, and is a fulcrum
for the subsequent ... b5 pawn
thrust.

   6 ♘5c3!?(35)

This should give Black little
trouble. The main line runs
**6 ♘d6+!** ♗×d6 7 ♕×d6 and
now:

a) **7 ... ♕f6** see chapters 1 and 2.

b) **7 ... ♕e7?!** 8 ♕d1! ♕b4+
9 ♘c3 ♘f6 10 ♗d3 and not 10 ...
d5? 11 a3 ♕a5 12 ♗d2± –
AHM.

Elian – Antemia, Romanian
Junior Ch 1971, went instead

**6 ♘5a3?!** ♗c5 **7** ♗e2 ♘ge7
**8 c4?** (8 00 and 9 ♔h1) 8 ... 00
**9 00 d6 10** ♔h1 f5! etc.

35
B

F21 **6 ...** ♗c5?
F22 **6 ...** ♘f6

a) **6 ... ♗b4** 7 a3 ♗a5 8 b4 ♗b6
9 ♗c4 ♘f6 10 00 h6 11 ♘d2
00 12 ♘d5± Venkatroman –
Rajagapalan, Madras 1952 –
perhaps the first game with 5 ... a6.
b) **6 ... b5** 7 ♘d5 ♘f6 8 ♘1c3
♘×d5 9 ♘×d5 ♖b8 10 ♗e3
♘b4 11 ♕h5 ♗d6 12 000 ♘×d5
13 ♖×d5 ♕c7 14 ♕g4 ♗f8 15
♔b1   d6=   Bednarski–Minić,
Budva 1963.
c) **6 ... ♗e7** (G) when:
c1) **7 g3!?** ♘f6 8 ♗g2 00 9 00 d6
10 h3 ♗d7 11 ♗e3 b5 12 ♘d2
♖c8 13 f4 ♘a5∓ (0–1, 65)
Kagan–Peretz, Netanya 1971.
c2) **7 ♗c4** ♘f6 8 00 00 9 ♗e3
(9 ♗g5 ♘×e4) 9 ... d6 10 h3 b5
11 ♗d5 ♗d7 12 ♘d2 ♖e8 13
♘b3 b4 14 ♘a4 ♖b8 15 c3
♘×d5 16 ed ♘a5 and Black has
Q-side counterplay – U.
c3) **7 ♘d5!** – V.

**F21**

**6 ...**          ♗c5?
**7** ♗c4

Or 7 ♗e3!? ♗×e3 8 fe ♘f6
9 ♗c4 ♕b6!? 10 00 ♕×b2 11
♕d6!? ♕×a1 12 ♖×f6 gf 13
♕×f6   with   complications;
Brazilsky – Tarasevich, Moscow
1960, continued 13 ... 00? 14
♕g5+ ♔h8 15 ♕f6+ ♔g8 16 h4
d5 17 h5±.

**7 ...**          ♘ge7

7 ... ♕h4? fails to 8 ♗×f7+!
e.g. 8 ... ♔d8 (8 ... ♔×f7 9
♕d5+) 9 00 ♘f6 10 g3 ♕h3
11 ♗g5± Faibisovich–Kapengut,
USSR Junior Ch 1963.

**8 00**          **00**
**9 ♘d5**          **b5**
**10** ♗b3±

Brazilsky – Goldblat, Moscow
1962; White has a strong grip on
the centre.

**F22**

**6 ...**          ♘f6
**7** ♗g5

Or 7 ♗c4 b5 8 ♗d5 b4 (8 ...
♗b7 is unclear – U.) 9 ♘e2
♘×d5 10 ed ♘b8 11 ♗e3 d6
12 a3 ba 13 ♘×a3 ♗d7 14 ♘c4
and not now 14 ... ♕h4?
(Faibisovich–A. Zaitsev, Leningrad 1962) 15 ♖a4±.

**7 ...**          ♗e7

Foguelman–Rossetto, Mar del
Plata 1958, went 7 ... ♗c5 8 ♗c4
h6 9 ♗×f6 ♕×f6 10 00 00 11
♘d2 d6 12 ♘d5 ♕h4 13 f3
♔h8=.

**8 ♗×f6**          ♗×f6

9 ♘d5        ♗g5

Or 9 ... 00 10 ♗e2 d6 11 00
♗e6 12 c3 ♗×d5 13 ♕×d5 ♕b6
14 ♕b3 ♕c5 15 ♖d1 ♖fd8 16
♗c4 ♖d7 (½–½, 41) Browne–
Peretz, Netanya 1971.

10 ♗c4

Or 10 ♘1c3 00 11 ♗d3 b5 12
a3 d6 13 h4 ♗h6 14 g4 g6 15
g5!? (1–0, 35) Stefanov–Antemia,
Romanian Junior Ch 1970.

10 ...         00
11 ♘1c3        b5
12 ♗b3         ♘d4=

Chistiakov – Utyatsky, Moscow
1961, continued 13 h4 ♗e7 (13 ...
♗×h4? 14 ♕h5) 14 ♘×e7+
♕×e7 15 ♘d5 ♕c5 16 ♖h3
♗b7! and Black stands all right
in the complications.

## Conclusion

5 ♘×c6 and the unusual knight
retreats cause Black no problems,
but against 5 ♘b5 there unfortunately appears to be nothing
better than 5 ... a6 leading to the
critical lines of chapters 1 and 2.

# 4  5 ... e5, Introduction

One of the least-understood variations of the Sicilian arises after 1 e4 c5 2 ♘f3 ♘c6 3 d4 cd 4 ♘×d4 ♘f6 5 ♘c3 e5(*36*). As in the 4 ... e5 lines, but in our opinion with more justification, Black believes he will compensate for the d5 'hole' by active piece play and (in some cases) threatening pawn advances. 'If it worked so easily,' remarked Gligorić in *Chess Life and Review* (1974) 'Black would play nothing but the Sicilian Defence'. Yet it is not so easy to support such a dismissive attitude to Lasker's variation by concrete continuations!

36
W

A 6 ♘b3
B 6 ♘de2

C 6 ♘f3
D 6 ♘db5!

a) **6 ♘f5?!** d5 7 ed ♗×f5 8 dc ♕×d1+ :

a1) **9 ♔×d1** bc 10 ♗a6 ♖b8 11 ♗d3 (11 ♗e3 ♖×b2) 11 ... ♗g6∓ Filipov–Ganchev, Sofia 1950.

a2) **9 ♘×d1** bc 10 ♘e3 ♗g6 11 ♗e2 ♗c5 12 ♗f3 ♖c8 13 00 00 14 ♖d1 ♗e4= – U.

b) **6 ♘×c6?!** bc:

b1) **7 ♗g5** ♖b8! 8 ♗×f6 ♕×f6 9 ♗c4 ♖×b2 10 ♗b3 ♗b4∓ Malmgren – Alekhine, Orebrö 1935.

b2) **7 ♗c4** ♗b4 8 ♗g5 h6 (8 ... ♗×c3+!? 9 bc ♕a5 – G) when:

b21) **9 ♗×f6** ♕×f6 10 ♕d3 00 11 00 d6 12 a3 ♗c5∓ – U.

b22) **9 ♗h4** g5 (9 ... ♕a5∓) 10 ♗g3 ♘×e4 (10 ... d6!?) 11 ♗×e5 ♕e7 12 00 (12 ♕d4? ♘×c3 13 bc ♗c5 14 ♕e4 d5∓∓) 12 ... ♗×c3= – U.

b23) **9 ♗d2** ♗×c3 10 ♗×c3 ♘×e4 11 ♕g4 (11 ♗×e5?? ♕a5+ Weiss–Grünfeld, 1946) 11 ... 00 12 ♕×e4 d5 13 ♕e2 dc is unclear – U.

**A**

### 6 ♘b3

This is a move quite often tried by club players meeting 5 ... e5 for the first time. It should give Black a very free game, except maybe in the main line where White gives up a pawn for complications.

6 ...                    ♗b4!

G suggests 6 ... ♗e7, meeting 7 ♗g5? by 7 ... ♘×e4, or 7 ♗c4 by 7 ... 00.

### 7 ♗c4!?

Others:

a) **7 ♗g5** (Kuzminikh) 7 ... h6 8 ♗×f6 ♗×c3+! 9 bc ♕×f6:

a1) **10 ♗e2** 00 11 00 d6 12 ♕d3 ♖d8 13 ♖fd1 ♗e6 14 ♗f3 ♖ac8∓ Kashlyak–Panchenko, USSR 1969.

a2) **10 ♗d3** ♘e7 11 ♘d2 00 12 c4 d6 13 ♘f1 b5!? (13 ... ♗e6= U) 14 cb d5 15 ♘g3 ♗b7 with complications; Marjanović – Urzica, European Junior Ch, Groningen 1972–3

b) **7 ♗d3** d5! 8 ed ♘×d5 9 ♗d2 ♗×c3! (9 ... ♘×c3 see Schlechter–Lasker, p. xi) 10 bc 00 11 00 f5 12 ♗c4 ♔h8 13 ♗×d5 (13 ♕e2!?) 13 ... ♕×d5 14 ♗e3 ♕c4 15 ♕d3 ♗e6∓ Rezende–Zinn, Siegen Olympiad 1970.

c) If **7 ♗d2** then 7 ... 00 is safest as the pressure on White's king's pawn becomes embarrassing to him. Immediately 7 ... ♗×c3 8 ♗×c3 ♘×e4 does not win a pawn because of 9 ♗×e5! ♘×e5 10 ♕d5.

7 ...                    ♘×e4!?

Or:

a) **7 ... d6!** 8 00 ♗e6= – G; critical lines now are 9 ♘d5!? or 9 ♕d3 first.

b) **7 ... 00** 8 00 (8 ♕d3 d5!=) 8 ... ♗×c3 9 bc ♘×e4 10 ♗a3 d6 (10 ... ♖e8 11 ♗×f7+ ♔×f7 12 ♕d5+) 11 ♕d3 ♗f5 12 ♖ae1 ♕h4 13 f4! ef 14 ♖×e4± Kopayev–Korchnoi, Leningrad 1952.

### 8 00

This is better than 8 ♗×f7+ (or 8 ♕d5 ♘d6) 8 ... ♔×f7 9 ♕d5+ ♔e8 10 ♕×e4 ♗×c3+ 11 bc d5 12 ♕e2 – Cafferty, *Spassky's 100 Best Games*. White's chances on the dark squares may be outweighed by Black's control of the light squares and centre after 12 ... 00 13 ♗a3 ♖f7 14 00 b6 – AHM.

8 ...                    ♘×c3
9 bc                    ♗e7

Cafferty recommends returning material, along classical principles, by 9 ... ♗×c3 10 ♕f3 d5! e.g. 11 ♗×d5 00 12 ♗×f7+ (12 ♖d1 ♘d4!) 12 ... ♖×f7 13 ♕×c3 with about equal chances. Then after 13 ... ♗f5 Black even has chances on the c-file, e.g. 14 ♗b2 ♖c8 15 ♖ad1 ♖d7 with an eventual ... ♘d4 in mind – AHM.

### 10 f4!±

a) **10 ... 00?!** 11 f5 b5? (11 ... d5

12 ♗×d5 ♘d4! 13 ♗e4 ♘×b3
14 cb – Cafferty) 12 ♗d5 ♗b7
13   ♕h5±± Spassky–Kajan,
Student Olympiad, Lyons 1955.
b) **10 ... d6** is better, e.g. 11 ♕h5
g6 12 ♕h6 (12 ♕f3 ♗e6!) 12 ...
♗f8 and 13 ... ♗g7 – Cafferty.

**B**

**6 ♘de2**(*37*)

R commented in 1956: 'There
is a lot to be said for this move
from the positional point of view,
as it accentuates the weakness of
d5 and f5 (after ♘g3). But the
question is, whether Black cannot
profit in a tactical way from the
(temporarily) rather unfortunate
position of White's pieces'.

6 ...                ♗c5!?

Others:

a) **6 ... d5!?** 7 ed ♘b4 8 ♗g5 9
a3?! (9 ♘g3±) 9 ... ♘g4! 10
♗×d8 ♗×f2+ forcing perpetual
check – U.

b) If **6 ... ♗b4**, M gives 7 ♗d2
00 8 ♘g3∓ and this is probably
the best that White can do, unless
7 a3 ♗a5 should be interpolated.

7 ♘g3              d6

Not 7 ... ♕b6 8 ♕d2! d6 (8 ...
♘g4 9 ♘d1 and 10 h3 – R, 1957)
9 ♘a4 ♕c7 10 ♘×c5 dc
(Müller) 11 ♗e2 ♘d4 12 ♗d1
and 13 c3± – Euwe.

8 ♗e2            a6

Others:

a) **8 ... h5** 9 ♗g5! ♕b6 10
♗×f6! ♗×f2+ 11 ♔f1 ♗×g3
12 hg gf 13 ♕×d6 ♘d4 14
♕×b6 ab 15 ♘d5± Teschner–
Richter, W. Berlin 1949.

b) **8 ... ♗e6** when:

b1) **9 ♘d5?** ♗×d5 (9 ... ♘d4!?
– Müller) 10 ed ♘e7 11 00
♘f×d5 12 ♗b5+ ♔f8∓ Kadiri–
Zinn, Lugano Olympiad 1968.

b2) **9 00** d5!? (9 ... a6 see text)
10 ♘h5! ♘×h5 11 ed ♗×d5 12
♕×d5 ♕×d5 13 ♘×d5 ♖d8
(S. Bernstein–Hearst, USA Ch
1954) 14 ♘c7+! ♔d7 15 ♘a6!
ba 16 ♗×h5± – Evans, *M.C.O.*
(10th ed.).

9 00              ♗e6

a) **10 ♗g5!?** h6 11 ♗×f6 ♕×f6
12 ♘d5 ♕d8 13 c3± Nikolov–
Pantaleev, Primorsko 1970.

b) **10 ♔h1** ♘d4 11 f4 ♘×e2+
12 ♕×e2 ♘g4 13 f5 ♕h4 14 h3
h5 15 ♖f3 ♗d7 16 ♗d2 is
unclear; Fletzer–Benner, corres
1953.

**C**

**6 ♘f3**(*38*)

6 ...                ♗b4!

Or 6 ... ♗e7 when:

a) **7 ♗c4** 00:

a1) **8 00** d6 9 ♕e2 ♗d7 10 ♗e3
♖c8 11 ♖fd1 ♔h8 12 a3 ♕e8

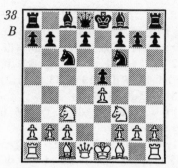

38
B

13 ♕f1 a6 14 ♖d2 b5∓ Turt-shanikov – Kuzminikh, USSR 1947.

a2) **8 ♗g5** d6 9 ♗×f6 ♗×f6 10 h3 ♗e6 11 ♗b3 ♕d7 12 00 ♗d8 13 ♕d3 ♗×b3 14 ab (14 cb!? – Gligorić) 14 ... ♘b4 15 ♕d2 ♕c6= Kopayev – Kuzminikh, USSR 1940.

b) R, 1961, suggested **7 ♗g5!** 00 8 ♗e2±. Compare chapter 8; this is a Boleslavsky in which Black has not yet played ... d6 and White is well placed to take control of d5.

  **7 ♗c4**

Ragozin's gambit attempt to improve upon:

a) **7 ♗d3** d5 e.g. 8 ♘d2 ♗×c3 9 bc 00∓ Atanasov–Hübner, Student Olympiad, Ybbs 1968.

b) **7 ♗g5** h6 8 ♗×f6 ♗×c3+ 9 bc ♕×f6 10 ♘d2 ♕g6 11 ♕f3 d6 12 ♗c4 00∓ Bordyansky–Gorelov, Moscow Spartakiad 1974.

  **7 ...** **00**

Others:

a) **7 ...** ♘×**e4?** 8 ♕d5 ♘d6 9 ♗b3± – Müller.

b) **7...** ♗×**c3+** 8 bc ♕a5–Euwe.

c) **7 ... d6** 8 00 ♗g4 (8 ... ♗e6!=; 8 ... 00 9 ♗g5) 9 ♘d5 ♘×d5 (9 ... ♘×e4? 10 ♘×b4 ♘×b4 11 ♕e1) 10 ed ♘e7! (10 ... ♘d4 11 c3! – R, 1957) 11 h3 ♗d7 12 ♗e3 f5 13 c3 ♗a5 14 ♘g5 f4 15 ♘e4 ♗f5 16 ♗d2± – U.

  **8 00!?**

Also:

a) **8 ♕d3?** d5 9 ♗×d5 ♘×d5 10 ♕×d5 ♕×d5 11 ed ♘d4 12 ♘×d4 ed 13 a3 ♗a5!∓ – G.

b) **8 ♗g5!?** ♕a5 (or 8 ... ♗×c3+ first) 9 ♗×f6 ♗×c3+ 10 bc ♕×c3+ 11 ♘d2 gf 12 ♖b1 with sufficient compensation–Ragozin. The question is whether, after 12 ... ♘d4, White can find anything better than the drawing line 13 ♕g4+ (13 00 d5!=) 13 ... ♔h8 14 ♕h4 etc.

  **8 ...** **d6**

8 ... ♗×c3 9 bc ♘×e4 allows White to get compensation for his pawn by 10 ♗a3 d6 11 ♕e1 ♗f5 12 ♖b1 ♕a5 13 ♘h4! although after 13 ... ♕×a3 (13 ... ♗c8? 14 ♗b4 Domnitz–Kchouk, Varna Olympiad 1962) 14 ♘×f5 ♘f6 Black's game seems playable.

  **9 ♘d5** **h6**

If 9 ... ♘×e4?! 10 ♘×b4 ♘×b4 11 ♕e1 d5 12 ♕×b4 dc 13 ♕×c4± – U.

  **10 ♘×b4** **♘×b4**
  **11 c3** **♘c6**
  **12 ♕d3**

M suggested 12 ♕e2!? and 13 ♖d1.

12 ...                     ♕c7
13 ♗b3                  ♘a5
14 ♗c2                  d5!=

Ortega–Zinn, Berlin 1968, continued 15 ♕e2 ♗g4 16 h3 (16 ed? e4 17 ♗×e4 ♖fe8) 16 ... ♗×f3 17 ♕×f3 and now correct (according to Uhlmann in *Informator*) would be 17 ... de! 18 ♕f5 ♕e7.

**D**

    **6 ♘db5!**(*39*)

The most forcing continuation, and probably the only real test of 5 ... e5.

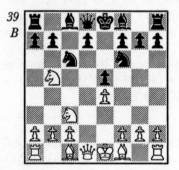

*39*
*B*

D1 6 ... h6!?
D2 6 ... d6!

a) **6 ... ♗c5** 7 ♗e3 (or 7 ♘d6+ ♔f8 8 ♗c4± – G) 7 ... ♗×e3?! 8 ♘d6+ ♔f8 9 fe ♕b6 10 ♘c4 ♕c5 11 ♕d6+ ♕×d6 12 ♘×d6 ♘e8 13 ♘cb5 ♘×d6 14 ♘×d6 ♘b4 15 000! ♘×a2+ 16 ♔b1 ♘b4 17 ♗c4±± Bivshev–Abramov, USSR 1951.

b) **6 ... ♗b4** 7 a3! ♗×c3+ (7 ... ♗e7 8 ♘d6+) 8 ♘×c3 d6 9 ♗g5 (9 ♘b5? ♘×e4 10 ♗d3 a6) 9 ...

h6 (9 ... a6 10 ♘d5 ♗e6 11 ♗×f6 gf 12 ♘e3±) 10 ♗×f6 ♕×f6 11 ♘b5 (or 11 ♘d5 ♕d8 12 ♗c4±) 11 ... 00 12 ♕×d6 ♕h4 13 ♕d3 (13 ♗d3 ♕g5!?) 13 ... ♖d8 14 ♕e3± – U.

c) **6 ... a6** 7 ♘d6+ ♗×d6 8 ♕×d6:

c1) **8 ... h6** 9 ♗e3 ♕e7 10 ♗c5 b5 11 ♘d5 ♘×d5 12 ed ♕×d6 13 ♗×d6 ♘d4 14 00 (eventually drawn in Hannah–Lowe, match game 1866!) is an historical curiosity.

c2) **8 ... ♕e7** when:

c21) **9 ♕d1** (G) 9 ... h6!:

c211) **10 ♘d5** ♘×d5 11 ed ♘d4 12 c3 ♘f5 13 ♗d3± (two bishops); or

c212) **10 ♗c4** d6 11 ♗e3 ♗e6 12 ♘d5!? ♗×d5 13 ed ♘b8!? 14 00± – U.

c22) **9 ♕×e7+** ♘×e7 (9 ... ♔×e7? 10 ♗g5 ♘b4 11 000 h6 12 ♗×f6+ ♔×f6 13 a3± – U) 10 ♗g5 h6 (10 ... d5 11 ♗×f6 gf 12 ♘×d5 ♘×d5 13 ed ♗f5 14 000±± – U) 11 ♗×f6 gf 12 g3 00 13 ♖d1 ♔g7 (13 ... f5 – Tartakower and du Mont) 14 ♗h3 d6 15 ♗×c8 ♘×c8 16 ♘d5± Griffith–Hammond, Richmond 1912.

**D1**

    **6 ...                     h6!?**

Haberditz introduced this move as an attempt to improve upon the last variation by preventing ♗g5, but it is not good enough.

    7 ♘d6+!

Others:

a) **7 ♗e3** d6 8 a4! ♗e6?! (but
8 ... ♗e7 9 ♘d5 ♘×d5 10 ed
♘b8 11 a5!) 9 ♘d5! ♗×d5
(9 ... ♖c8 10 ♘×f6 gf 11 c4) 10
ed ♘e7 11 a5! ♘c8 (or 11 ...
♘e×d5 12 ♗×a7 ♗e7 13 c4
♘b4 14 ♖a4!) 12 a6 ba 13
♖×a6 ♗e7 14 c4 00 15 c5!±
Karklins–Martz, USA Ch 1973.
b) **7 ♘d5** ♘×d5 8 ed a6 (8 ...
♘b4 9 d6!) when:
b1) **9 dc** ab 10 cd+ (10 cb ♗b7
11 ♕e2 ♕c7! – U) 10 ... ♗×d7
(Orienter–Haberditz,  Vienna
1952) 11 ♗d3 (or 11 ♕e2!
♕c7!? – *Informator* 2) 11 ... ♗c6
12 00 ♕d5 13 ♕g4 h5 ($\frac{1}{2}$–$\frac{1}{2}$, 18)
Vitolins–Lutikov, USSR 1970.
b2) **9 ♘c3** ♘d4 10 ♗d3 d6 11 00
g6 12 ♘e4 ♗g7 (Johansson–
Bilek, Czechoslovakia 1968) 13
a4!? 00 14 ♘g3± – Hort.
c) **7 ♗c4** (Rabar–Haberditz,
Vienna 1953) 7 ... a6! 8 ♘d6+
♗×d6 9 ♕×d6 ♕e7 10 ♕×e7+
(10 ♕c7 d5! 11 ♕×e7+ ♘×e7
12 ed ♗f5= – U) 10 ... ♔×e7
11 ♗e3 d6 12 000 ♗e6=
Karpov–Hug, Student Olympiad,
Graz 1972.

    7 ...        ♗×d6
    8 ♕×d6    ♕e7(*40*)
D11 9 ♘b5!
D12 9 ♕×e7+

a) **9 ♕d1** 00 10 ♗e3 ♖d8 11 a3
d6 12 ♗e2 ♗e6 13 ♘d5 ♗×d5
14 ed ♘d4= Schalk–Haberditz,
Vienna 1950.
b) **9 ♕d2?!** 00 10 ♗c4 d6 11 b3

♗e6 12 ♗×e6 fe 13 ♗a3? (13
♕b2) 13 ... ♘d4∓ Honfi–Bilek,
Kecskemet 1972.

**D11**
    **9 ♘b5!**    ♕×d6

Best, since 9 ... ♘×e4? 10
♘c7+ costs the exchange, and
9 ... 00 10 ♕×e7 ♘×e7 11 ♘d6
makes it even harder for Black to
free his game – Gligorić, *Chess
Life and Review*.

    10 ♘×d6+    ♔e7
    11 ♘f5+    ♔f8

Milić had given this as equal in
*Informator* 3, thinking that White
must guard his e-pawn, but ...

    12 b3!    d5

After 12 ... ♘×e4 13 ♗a3+
♔g8 14 ♘d6 ♘×d6 15 ♗×d6
Black's development would be
paralyzed – Gligorić.

    13 ♗a3+    ♔g8
    14 ed    ♘×d5

If 14 ... ♘d4 15 ♘e7+.

    15 ♘d6    ♖b8
    16 ♗c4    ♗e6
    17 000±

The  model  game  Spassky–
Gheorghiu, European Team Ch,

Bath 1973, continued 17 ... ♘f4
(17 ... ♘c3 18 ♗×e6 fe 19 ♖de1)
18 g3 ♗×c4 19 ♘×c4 (threatening 20 ♖d7) 19 ... ♘e2+ 20
♔b2! b5 21 ♖he1 bc (21 ...
♘ed4 22 ♘×e5 b4 23 ♗×b4!
♖×b4 24 c3±) 22 ♖×e2 f6 23
♖e4! cb 24 cb! ♔h7 25 ♖c4
♖hd8 (25 ... ♘d4 26 ♗c5 ♖fc8
27 ♖1c1 or 26 f4) 26 ♖×d8
♘×d8 27 ♗c5! a6 28 ♔c3 ♔g6
29 a4 ♔f7 30 ♗e3 ♔e6 31 ♖c7!
♖b7 32 ♖c8! ♖d7 33 ♗b6!
♘b7 34 ♖a8 ♖d6 35 a5 ♖c6+
36 ♔b4 ♘d6 37 ♖×a6 ♘c8 38
♔b5 ♔d5 39 ♖a8 ♖c3 40 ♔b4
♖c2 41 ♗e3 1-0.

**D12**

9 ♕×e7+     ♔×e7 (41)

41
W

D121 10 b3
D122 10 ♗e3!

**D121**

**10 b3**        d6
  11 ♗a3        ♖d8
  Or 11 ... a6 (11 ... ♗e6!? – U)
12 ♗d3!? ♗e6 13 00 b5 14 ♘d1
♖hb8 15 ♘e3 a5= Lutikov–
Vasyukov, USSR 1968.

  12 000        ♗e6

Others:
a) **12 ... ♘d4?** 13 f4 ♔e8
(Haberditz) 14 ♗×d6! – Estrin.
b) **12 ... a6!?** 13 ♘d5+ ♘×d5
14 ed ♘b8 15 ♗d3± – B.
    13 ♘d5+!     ♗×d5
    14 ed        ♘b8!
    Not 14 ... ♘d4? 15 f4!±±.
    15 ♖e1
    Or 15 ♗d3 a5! 16 ♖he1
♘fd7! 17 f4 f6 18 ♖e3 ♘a6 19
♖g3 g5 20 fg hg 21 h4 ♘b4!
22 hg fg 23 ♔b2 (23 ♖×g5?
♖g8) 23 ... ♘c5!= Holmov–
Ciocaltea, Tbilisi 1970.
    15 ...        ♘fd7

Others:
a) **15 ... ♔d7** 16 f4 ef 17 ♗b5+
♔c7 18 ♖e7+ Zuckerman–
Sherwin, New York 1967.
b) **15 ... ♘bd7** 16 f4± – Milić
c) **15 ... ♖d7** (15 ... ♘g4 16 f4
and 17 h3) 16 ♖×e5+ ♔d8 17
♖e3 ♘×d5 18 ♖d3± – AHM.
    16 f4         f5
    17 h4!±
Tringov–Gheorghiu, Bulgaria v.
Romania 1972.

**D122**

    10 ♗e3!       d6
    11 f3
    A necessary precaution against
... ♘g4.
    11 ...         ♗e6
    Or 11 ... a6 12 000 b5 (Mednis–
Lombardy, New York 1969) 13
a4! b4 14 ♘d5+ ♘×d5 15 ed
♘a5 16 ♗b6 ♘b7 17 a5± –
Byrne.
    12 000        ♖fd8

Others:

a) **12 ... a6** 13 ♗e2 ♖ac8 14 ♖d2± Radulov–Drimer, Havana 1969.

b) **12 ... ♖he8** 13 g4 a6 14 h4 ♘d7 15 ♖h2!± Tukmakov–Dzhindzhihasvili, USSR 1968.

c) **12 ... ♖hc8** 13 ♔b1 a6 14 ♘a4 ♘d7 15 c4 ♘a7± Kavalek–Soos, Polanica Zdroj 1968.

13 g4

Or 13 a3 ♘a5 14 b3 ♖ac8 15 ♔b2 b6 16 ♘b5 ♖d7 17 c4 (1–0, 43) Suetin–Kliavin, Minsk ½-final, 25th USSR Ch 1957.

    13 ...            ♖ac8
    14 h4            ♘e8
    15 ♖h2          a6

16 g5 hg 17 hg b5 18 ♗b6! ♖d7 19 ♘d5+ ♗×d5 20 ed ♖b7 21 ♗e3 ♘b8 22 f4± Stein–Miagmasuren, Sousse interzonal 1967.

**D2**

    **6 ...            d6!**(42)

Now the white ♘b5 is somewhat offside and must be redeployed via a3. Black reckons that this will give him the time

42
W

to forestall White's plans to dominate d5.

D21 7 ♘d5!?

D22 7 a4!?

D23 7 ♗e3!?

a) **7 ♗g5** is usual; then:

a1) **7 ... a6** 8 ♗×f6 chapter 5. According to the 8th edition of the *Handbuch des Schachspiels*, Tartakower recommended this line – before the first World War! 

a2) **7 ... a6** 8 ♘a3 chapter 6.

a3) **7 ... ♗e6** 8 ♘d5 (8 ♗×f6 gf 9 ♘d5 – AHM) 8 ... ♗×d5 9 ed ♘e7 10 ♘c3 (10 ♗×f6 gf 11 c4 f5 12 ♕h5± – B) 10 ... ♘d7 11 ♗e2 h6 12 ♗h4 a6 13 ♕d2!? ♕b6 14 f3 ♖c8 15 ♘a4 (Ivanov–Bukhman, USSR 1967) 15 ... ♕d4!? with an unclear position – Yudovich, *Informator* 4.

b) **7 ♘a3** ♗e6 (7 ... ♗e7 8 ♗g5 ♘×e4?! 9 ♗×e7±) 8 ♗g5 ♖c8 and Black has not needed to spend a tempo on ... a6; Gavaleshvili–Timoshenko, USSR 1974.

**D21**

    **7 ♘d5!?        ♘×d5**
    **8 ed            ♘b8**

8 ... ♘e7 9 c4 ♘f5 is not so reliable.

    **9 c4**

If 9 ♗e3 a6 10 ♘c3 ♘d7 11 ♕d2 ♗e7 12 f4 f5 13 ♗d3 OO and Black is in no trouble; Sarwinski–Bielczyk, Poland 1973.

    **9 ...            a6**

G recommends 9 ... ♗e7. Is 10 c5 a6 (10 ... dc? 11 d6) 11 cd playable then?

10 ♘c3      ♗e7
11 ♗d3

Or 11 ♗e2 00 12 00 f5 13 b4 ♘d7 with similar play (0–1, 35); Judycki–Bielczyk, Poland 1971.

11 ...      00
12 00       ♘d7

M suggested 12 ... f5!?, which indeed seems the natural choice. These positions with rival pawn majorities are never easy to evaluate.

After 12 ... ♘d7, Lein–Minev, Novi Sad 1972, continued 13 ♕c2! g6 14 ♗h6 ♖e8 15 ♗e3 f5 16 f3 ♗f6 (= U) 17 ♖ae1 ♗g7 18 ♔h1 ♖f8 19 ♕e2 and now Minev said he should have played 19 ... g5, threatening 20 ... e4 21 fe f4, with an unclear position.

**D22**

**7 a4!? (43)**

Suggested by Schlechter in the *Wiener Schachzeitung* (1910) in notes to his game with Lasker, this move was later recommended also by Alekhine. However Larsen is right in saying that 'few masters will prefer this to 7 ♗g5';

43
B

its consequences remain relatively unexplored.

D221 7 ... h6?!
D222 7 ... ♗e6
D223 7 ... a6

7 ... ♗e7 is a little passive:

a) **8 ♗e2?** 00 9 ♗e3 ♗c6 10 ♘d5 ♘×e4 11 ♘×e7+ ♕×e7 12 f3 a6!∓ Grigoriev–Nenarokov, Moscow 1921.

b) **8 ♗c4** a6 9 ♘a3 ♗e6 10 ♗g5± – M.

**D221**

**7 ...      h6?!**
**8 ♗c4**

Another crucial line is 8 ♘a3 (8 ♗e3 a6) 8 ... ♗e6 9 ♗c4 ♗×c4 10 ♘×c4 ♘×e4 11 ♘×e4 d5 12 ♘×e5 ♘×e5 13 ♘g3 ♗c5 (½–½, 59) Ljubojević–Tal, Wijk aan Zee 1976.

8 ...       a6

Or 8 ... ♗e6 9 ♘d5 ♖c8 (½–½, 49) Onoprienko – Panchenko, RSFSR Spartakiad 1975.

9 ♘a3       ♗e6
10 ♗d5      ♖c8

11 00 ♗×d5 (11 ... ♗e7 12 ♘c4) 12 ♘×d5! (12 ed ♘b4) 12 ... ♘×e4 (more careful 12 ... ♗e7 or 12 ... ♘×d5) 13 ♘c4 ♘f6 14 ♘×f6+ ♕×f6 15 ♘b6 ♖b8 16 ♘d5 ♕d8 (Gipslis–Timoshenko, Moscow 1975) 17 ♖a3± – Gipslis.

**D222**

**7 ...      ♗e6**
**8 ♗g5      a6**
Others:
a) **8 ... ♗e7?** 9 ♗×f6 gf 10 ♘d5

♗g5 11 c3 a6 12 ♘a3 f5 13 ef ♗×f5 14 ♘c4± Hennings–Lorenz, Leipzig 1971.

b) **8 ... ♖c8!?** 9 ♗×f6 gf 10 ♘d5 ♗×d5 (10 ... f5 11 ♘bc3!±) 11 ed5 ♘e7 12 ♘c3 (Pavlov – Marcovici, Iaşi 1975) 12 ... a6! 13 ♗d3 f5 14 g4= – Pavlov.

     9 ♘a3         ♖c8
    10 ♘c4

Or 10 ♗c4 ♗e7 11 00 00 12 ♗×f6 ♗×f6 13 ♘d5! ♗g5 14 c3 ♘e7!?)14 ... ♔h8= Hennings – Pavlov, Bucharest 1971) 15 ♕b3!± Balinas – Ciocaltea, Nice Olympiad 1974.

    10 ...         ♘d4
    11 ♘e3

Or 11 ♗×f6 (11 ♘d5 ♗×d5!) 11 ... ♕×f6 12 ♘e3 d5 13 ed ♗b4 14 ♗c4 ♗f5 15 00 ♗g6 16 ♘g4 ♕f4 17 ♘e3 (Savon–Tseshkovsky, USSR zonal play-off 1975) 17 ... ♘×c2! with an unclear position.

    11 ...         ♗e7
    12 ♗×f6     ♗×f6
    13 ♗d3      ♗g5

14 ♘ed5 00 (intending ... g6 and ... f5) with balanced chances; M. Kovacs–Zinn, Baja 1971.

**D223**

    7 ...         a6
    8 ♘a3(*44*)    ♗e6

8 ... d5!? is interesting:

a) **9 ♗g5** d4 10 ♘d5 ♗e6 11 ♗c4 ♗×d5 12 ed ♗b4+ 13 ♔f1 ♘a5 14 ♕e2 ♕d6 15 ♗×f6 ♕×f6 16 ♗b5+ ♔f8 17 ♗d3 g6

18 ♘c4 ♘×c4 19 ♗×c4 ♖c8 20 h4 h6= Letelier–Rossetto, Mar del Plata 1958.

b) **9 ed ♘d4** (not 9 ... ♗×a3 10 ♖×a3) 10 ♗c4 (10 ♗e3 looks stronger.) 10 ... ♗×f5, threatening ... ♗×a3 and ... ♘×c2+ – U.

    9 ♗c4      ♖c8

Others:

a) **9 ... ♘b4** 10 00 ♖c8= – U.

b) **9 ... ♗e7** 10 00 (10 ♗g5 00 11 ♗×f6! below) 10 ... 00 and not now 11 ♗g5? ♘×e4! (Grünfeld) but 11 h3 or 11 f3 and 12 ♗e3± – R, 1956.

c) Not **9 ... ♗×c4?!** 10 ♘×c4? ♘×e4? because of 11 ♘×e4 d5 12 ♗g5! f6 13 ♗×f6 gf 14 ♕×d5!±± Gaprindashivili – Polihroniade, Women's Olympiad, Medellin 1974.

    10 00

Or 10 ♗g5 see D222.

    10 ...        ♗e7

Müller's 10 ... ♘b4 is dubious, e.g. 11 ♗×e6 (or 11 ♘d5 –R, 1956) 11 ... fe 12 f4 ♗e7 13 ♕e2 ♕c7 14 ♗e3 Drimer–Sørensen, Whitby 1967.

    11 ♗g5

Or 11 ♗e3 00= Reinhardt–
Pelikan, Argentine Ch 1961.

11 ...          00
12 ♗×f6          ♗×f6

'White has a strategically better
position' – G. The critical line
runs 13 ♘d5 ♗g5 14 c3 ♚h8:
a) **15 f4!?** ♘a5!? with complications; Hartmann – Bielczyk,
Poland 1973 (0–1, 31);
b) **15** ♕e2 (one idea now is 16
b4) 15 ... ♗e7?! (15 ... ♘a5 –
AHM) 16 ♘×e7 ♕×e7 17
♖ad1 ♖fd8 18 ♗×e6 fe 19 c4
(1–0, 56) Hennings–Pavlov,
Bucharest 1971.

**D23**

**7 ♗e3!?** *(45)*

This line is quite important as
it can be (and usually is) reached
by other move-orders, viz. 1 e4
c5 2 ♘f3 ♘c6 3 d4 cd 4 ♘×d4
♘f6 5 ♘c3 d6 6 ♗e3 e5 7 ♘db5
or the Taimanov variation
sequence 1 e4 c5 2 ♘f3 e6 3 d4
cd 4 ♘×d4 ♘c6 5 ♘b5 d6 6 ♗f4
e5 7 ♗e3 a6 8 ♘5c3 ♘f6 9 ♘a3
(both sides having lost a move)
which is discussed further on
page xv.

45
B

7 ...          a6

7 ... ♗e7!? was recommended
in *The Sicilian Sozin* (p. 178),
following R, 1956, but it may not
be good, after all:
a) **8** ♕d2 a6 9 ♘a3 b5 and not
10 ♘d5? since the queen is en
prise after 10 ... ♘×e4.
b) **8** ♗g5 a6 9 ♗×f6 (9 ♘a3?
♘×e4!) 9 ... gf 10 ♘a3 and
Black has gained a tempo on
some lines in chapter 5.
c) **8** ♘d5 ♘×d5 9 ed ♘b8 is
critical. R now commented: '...
followed by ... 00 and if possible
... f5. We know from the normal
Boleslavsky variation that positions of this kind are certainly not
unfavourable to Black.' But Euwe,
in his book on the Sicilian, subsequently recommended 10 ♕d2!,
a superb 'creeping move' which,
by ruling out ... ♕a5+, creates
a strong threat of ♘×a7. The
best defence is 10 ... a6 (10 ... f5
11 f4! or 10 ... b6 11 a4! 00 12
a5! – AHM) 11 ♘a3 f5 (11 ... b5
12 c4± – Euwe) followed by ...
♘d7, but further investigation is
needed to determine whether this
will be adequate. Clearly White
has a strong Q-side grip, but
Black's K-side chances are not
negligible.

8 ♘a3          ♖b8

Plausible alternatives:
a) **8 ... b5** 9 ♘d5 when:
a1) **9 ...** ♘×**d5** 10 ed ♘e7! 11 c4
♘f5 (Konstantinopolsky suggested 11 ... b4!? 12 ♕a4+ ♗d7.)

12 cb!? (12 ♘c2!?) 12 ... ♘×e3
13 fe ♕h4+ 14 g3 ♕e4 15 ♕c2!
♕×e3+ (15 ... ♕×h1 16
♕c6+) 16 ♗e2 ♗d7 17 ba ♗e7
18 ♕d2 ♕×d2+ (18 ... ♕a7 19
♘b5± Kotkov–Krogius, Sverdlovsk 1958) 19 ♔×d2 ♗g5+ 20
♔e1 ♗c8? (20 ... ♔e7! –
Kotkov) 21 ♘c4 ♔e7 (21 ...
♖×a6 22 b4! ♗d7? 23 ♘×e5)
and now instead of 22 ♘a5?
(½-½, 55 in Kotkov–Taimanov,
RSFSR Ch 1960) Kotkov gave
22 ♘b6! ♖a7 23 ♘×c8 24 b4±.
a2) **9 ... ♖b8** 10 ♘×f6+ (10
♗e2 ♗e7! – Nikitin) 10 ...
♕×f6 11 ♘b1 (11 c4 b4∓ –
Botterill) 11 ... ♗b7 12 ♘c3
♘d4! 13 ♗×d4 (13 a3 g6 14 ♕d2
♗g7 15 000 00= – B) 13 ... ed
14 ♘d5 ♗×d5= Shianovsky–
Polugayevsky, USSR Team Ch
1962.
b) **8 ... d5!?** 9 ♘×d5 (9 ed!?
♗×a3 is unclear.) 9 ... ♘×e4
10 ♗b6 ♗c5! (Lee – del Corral,
Clare Benedict Teams, Brunnen
1966) e.g. 11 ♗×d8 ♗×f2+ 12
♔e2 ♗g4+ 13 ♔d3 ♘c5+ and
14 ... ♗×d1.
c) **8 ... ♗e6** 9 ♘c4 ♗e7 10 ♘b6
♖b8 11 ♘bd5± Lee–Cornelis,
Lugano Olympiad 1968.

9 ♗g5
White is a tempo (... ♖b8)
down on main lines, but 9 ♘d5
(or 9 ♘c4 b5) 9 ... ♘×d5 10 ed
♘e7 11 c4 ♘f5 is also excellent
for Black–Nikitin.

9 ...            ♗e6
Or 9 ... b5 10 ♘d5 ♕a5+ 11
♗d2 ♕d8 12 ♘×f6+ ♕×f6
13 ♗d3 ♗e7 14 00 00 15 c4 ♘d4
16 cb ab 17 ♘c2= Bivshev–
Taimanov, USSR 1962.
10 ♘c4         b5
11 ♘e3         ♗e7
12 ♗×f6        ♗×f6
13 ♘cd5 ♗g5 14 ♗e2 00 15 00
g6 16 a4 f5 17 ab ab 18 ef gf with
two bishops and powerful pawns
for Black (0–1, 36); Kuindzhi–
Vasyukov, USSR 1st League Ch
1973.

Conclusion
Only 6 ♘db5 poses a serious
threat, when after 6 ... d6 (the
only sound move) White's best
move is almost certainly 7 ♗g5
as in chapters 5 and 6. However,
7 ♘d5, 7 a4 and 7 ♗e3 all lead
to unbalanced positions offering
chances to both players and
improvements may be possible in
all these lines.

# 5  5 ... e5, 8 ♗ × f6

The most common line against the Lasker Variation is 1 e4 c5 2 ♘f3 ♘c6 3 d4 cd 4 ♘ × d4 ♘f6 5 ♘c3 e5 6 ♘db5 d6 7 ♗g5 a6 8 ♗ × f6 gf 9 ♘a3 (*46*), at which point Black has a major choice to make.

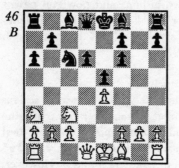

*46*
*B*

A 9 ... d5
B 9 ... b5
C 9 ... f5
D 9 ... ♗e6

Each of these moves, in different ways, contest White's hold on the central white squares c4, d5, f5 etc., and each has its own special advantages and drawbacks. The current fashion is to play ... b5 and/or ... f5 rather than the older lines with ... d5.

## A
**9 ...　　　　d5**

This pawn sacrifice is the Pelikan Variation. Black exposes the weak side of the white ♘a3, and seeks to eliminate, at a trivial cost, the long-term weakness on the d-file.

10 ♘ × d5

Others are risky:

a) **10 ♕ × d5** ♗e6! (10 ... ♕c7 11 ♕d2! – R, 1957) 11 ♕ × d8+ ♖ × d8:

a1) **12 ♗d3** ♗b4! 13 ♘c4 ♗ × c3+ 14 bc ♔e7= – M.

a2) **12 ♘c4** ♗b4 (12 ... ♗h6!? – Parma) with ample compensation for the pawn, according to Pelikan himself. Planinc–Benko, Sarajevo 1970, continued 13 ♘e3 ♔e7 14 ♗d3 ♗ × c3+ 15 bc ♘a5 16 00 ♖c8 17 f4 ♘c4= and Black even won after an error by his opponent.

b) **10 ed** ♗ × a3:

b1) **11 dc** ♗ × b2 12 ♕ × d8+ ♔ × d8 13 ♖d1+ ♔c7∓ – M.

b2) **11 ba** ♕a5 12 ♕d2 ♘d4 (∓ – Pelikan) 13 ♗d3 ♗h3!:

b21) **14 00??** ♘f3+! 15 gf ♖g8+

16 ♔h1 ♗g2+ 17 ♔g1 ♗×f3+ etc.

b22) **14 ♗e4** f5 15 gh fe 16 ♔f1 f5 17 ♖b1 000 18 ♖g1 ♖hg8∓ (0–1, 25) Drozdov–Ussakovsky, Moscow Central Chess Club Ch 1972.

b23) **14 ♔f1!?** ♘f3!? 15 ♕e3! (Tustikayev–Arutinian, USSR 1975) is unclear.

    10 ...        ♗×a3

    11 ba        ♗e6

Not 11 ... ♖g8 12 ♗c4 ♖×g2 13 ♕h5 – R, 1957.

    12 ♗c4

Others:

a) **12 ♕d2?** f5 13 f3 fe 14 fe ♕h4+ 15 ♔d1 000 16 ♗d3 f5 17 ♘c3 fe 18 ♘×e4 ♖d4 19 g3 ♕e7 20 ♕c3 ♗d5 21 ♖e1 ♔b8 22 ♔c1 ♖c8 23 ♘c5 ♗c4! 24 ♘b3 ♖×d3! 25 ♕×c4 (25 cd? ♗×b3) 25 ... ♕×a3+ 26 ♔b1 ♖d7 27 ♕e2 ♖d5 28 c3 ♘a5 29 ♕b2 ♕d6 30 ♘×a5 ♖×a5 31 a4 ♖d5 32 ♖c1 ♖d2 33 ♖c2 ♕d3 34 ♖a3 ♖f8 35 ♖b3 ♖f1+ 36 ♔a2 ♖×c2 0–1 (37 ♖b8+ ♔c8) A. Phillips–Markland, Hastings Challengers 1969–70.

b) **12 ♘e3!?** ♕a5+ 13 ♕d2 ♕×a3 14 ♗d3 000 15 00 when:

b1) **15 ...** **♖hg8** (15 ... ♖d7? 16 ♘d5±) 16 ♖fb1 (16 ♘d5?! ♗×d5 17 ed ♘d4!) 16 ... ♖d7 17 ♔h1 (17 ♘d5!?) 17 ... ♖gd8 18 ♕e1 ♖d4 19 ♕f1 ♕c3 20 a3 ♔c7?! 21 f4!± Geller–Pilnik, Amsterdam Candidates' 1956.

b2) Pilnik later suggested **15 ...**

♖d4!∓ with pressure on the d-file, e.g. 16 ♘d5 ♗×d5 17 ed (hoping for 17 ... ♖×d5? 18 ♗f5+) 17 ... ♘b4! – R.

b3) R also suggested **15 ... ♔b8** (preventing ♘d5) and 15 ... ♘b4!?=.

    12 ...        ♕a5+

    13 ♕d2 (47)

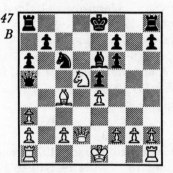

A1 13 ... ♕×d2+

A2 13 ... 000

**A1**

    13 ...        ♕×d2+

    14 ♔×d2    000

    15 ♖ad1

Or:

a) **15 ♗b3** f5 16 ♔c3 ♘d4 17 ♖ad1 fe= Tukmakov–R. Garcia, Buenos Aires 1970.

b) **15 ♔e3!?** ♘a5 (15 ... f5!?) 16 ♗b3 (16 ♘b6+!?) 16 ... ♘×b3 17 ab ♗×d5 18 ed ♖×d5 19 ♖hd1 ♖hd8= Ivashin–Golichov, USSR 1956.

    15 ...        f5

Or 15 ... ♖hg8:

a) **16 ♖hg1?** f5 17 ♔c3 fe 18 ♘b6+ ♔c7∓ Sznapik–Bielczyk, Poland 1969.

b) **16 g3** b5 17 ♗d3 f5 18 ♔c1 fe 19 ♗×e4 f5 20 ♗g2 ♖g7 Behrensen-Pelikan, Argentine Ch 1955.

16 f3!

16 ♔c1 allows:

a) **16 ...** **♖hg8** 17 g3 fe= Najdorf-Pelikan, Argentine Ch 1955; or

b) **16 ... fe** 17 ♘b6+ ♔c7 18 ♗×e6 (Jasnikowski-Bielczyk, Poland 1973) 18 ... ♔×b6= − Bielczyk, *The Chess Player* 6.

16 ...            ♖hg8

A line worth testing is 16 ... fe 17 fe f5! 18 ♔e3 (± − U) 18 ... f4+= − M.

17 g3            ♔b8!?

18 ♔e3±

Stein-Benko, Caracas 1970, continued 18 ... ♘d4 19 ♗b3 fe 20 fe f5 21 ♘e7 f4+ 22 gf ef+ 23 ♔×f4 ♖gf8+ 24 ♘f5 ♗×f5 25 ef ♖×f5+ 26 ♔e4 ♖h5 27 h4 ♘c6 28 ♖×d8+ ♘×d8 29 ♔f4 ♔c7 30 ♔g4 ♖e5 31 ♖f1 31 ♖f1 h5+ 32 ♔f4 ♖c5 33 ♖g1 ♔d6 34 ♖g5 ♖c3 35 ♖×h5 ♘e6+ 36 ♔e4 1–0.

**A2**

**13 ...            000**

14 ♖d1

Or 14 ♕×a5 ♘×a5 15 ♗b3 ♘×b3 16 ab ♗×d5 17 ed ♖×d5 18 ♔e2 ♖g8 ½–½ Hasin-Spassky, Leningrad ½-final, 24th USSR Ch 1956.

14 ...            ♕×a3

15 00            ♖hg8?!

We think 15 ... ♘d4 gives more chances.

16 ♕e3!            ♕×e3

17 fe            ♔b8

Or 17 ... ♖g4 18 ♗d3 f6 19 ♘f6 ♖h4 20 ef ♗×f5 21 ♗e4± Shamkovich-Jongsma, Amsterdam 1968.

18 ♗b3            ♖g6

19 ♘b6            ♔c7

20 ♖×d8            ♘×d8

21 ♘d5+ ♗×d5 22 ♗×d5 ♘e6 23 h4! h5 24 ♖f5± Fischer-Rossetto, Buenos Aires 1960.

**B**

**9 ...            b5**

10 ♘d5

Not 10 ♘a×b5? ab 11 ♗×b5 ♗d7 12 ♕h5 ♘e7 13 ♗c4 ♘g6 (Sahs) 14 f4 ef 15 ♕d5 ♘e5∓∓ − U.

10 ...            f5!? (*48*)

10 ... ♗e6 11 c3! e.g.:

a) **11 ...** ♖g8 12 ♘c2 ♗h6 13 a4! ♗×d5 14 ♕×d5 ♘e7 15 ♕d3 ba 16 ♖×a4 a5 17 ♘a3± Bhend-Kinzel, Venice 1953.

b) **11 ... f5** 12 ef!±.

c) **11 ... ♗g7** 12 ♘c2 f5 13 ef ♗×f5 14 ♘ce3 ♗g6 15 a4± when:

c1) **15 ...** ♖b8 16 ab ab 17 ♖a6 ♕c8 18 ♔a1 (1–0, 49) Ivkov-Puc, Yugoslav Ch 1949.

c2) **15 ... b4** 16 ♘×b4 ♘×b4 17 cb 00 18 b5± Barczay-Radojević, Sombor 1966.

The text move, first played by Shamkovich in 1955, was revived by young Soviet masters Sveshnikov and Timoshenko in 1973. Although two or three lines seem dangerous to Black, the complications are such that one can never be sure that the last word has been said.

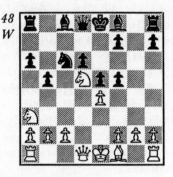

48
W

From diagram 48:
B1 11 ♗×b5!?
B2 11 ♗d3
B3 11 ef
or:
a) **11 ♘×b5?!** ab 12 ♗×b5 (hoping for 12 ... ♕a5+ ? 13 b4!) 12 ... ♗d7∓.
b) **11 g3!?** (11 ♕h5 fe∓) 11 ... fe 12 ♗g2 ♗g7! (Kondratiev, *Informator* 15) 13 ♗×e4 ♖a7! is unclear – U.
c) **11 c4** when:
c1) **11 ... ♕a5+** 12 ♕d2 ♕×d2+ 13 ♔×d2 ♔d8 14 cb ab 15 ♘×b5 fe with complications; Karasin–Abramov, Moscow 1966;
c2) **11 ... b4!** 12 ♘c2 fe 13 ♘c×b4 (or 13 ♘d×b4 ♘×b4 14 ♘×b4 ♕a5 15 ♕d2 ♖b8 with good play) 13 ... ♘d4 14 ♗e2 ♗g7 15 ♗g4 ♗×g4 16 ♕×g4 00!∓ Harding–F. Huguet, Monte Carlo 1968.

**B1**

**11 ♗×b5!?** ab
12 ♘×b5 ♖a7

The only move to have been tried, although 12 ... ♖b8 (12 ... ♕a5+ 13 c3) 13 ♘bc7+ ♔d7 may not be a forced win for White.

13 ♘×a7 ♘×a7
14 ♕f3

Others:
a) **14 c3** ♘c6 15 000? (15 ♕f3 below) 15 ... ♗h6+ 16 ♔b1 fe 17 ♕×e4 00∓ Peresipkin–Sveshnikov, USSR Young Masters' Ch, Kiev 1973.
b) **14 ef!?**, suggested by Uhlmann, has not been played in any of the major games with the variation, but may be best. If 14 ... ♗×f5 15 ♕f3±.

14 ... ♘c6
15 c3 f4
16 g3

Probably improving upon 16 00 ♗g7 17 b4 00 18 ♕d3 ♘e7 19 c4 ♘×d5 20 ♕×d5 f3 (½–½, 54) of Sveshnikov – Timoshenko, USSR Young Masters' Ch, Cheliabinsk 1974.

16 ... h5
17 a4 ♗g7
18 a5 ♗a6

Sveshnikov – Sukhikh, ½-final USSR Armed Forces Ch 1975; the position is completely obscure (but 1–0, 43 – White being the stronger player).

**B2**

**11 ♗d3** ♗e6(*49*)

49
W

12 ♕h5

If 12 00 ♗g7 13 c4!? Browne–Dvoretsky, Wijk aan Zee 1976, went 13 ... bc 14 ♘×c4 00 15 ♘cb6 fe 16 ♗×e4 ♖b8 17 ♗×h7+ ♔×h7 18 ♕c2+ f5 19 ♕×c6 f4 ½–½.

Or 12 c3 ♗g7 13 00 00:

a) **14 ♘c2** ♖c8 15 ♘bc4 ♘×b4 16 ♘×b4 fe 17 ♗×e4 a5 18 ♘d5 f5 19 ♗c2 ♖c5 20 ♘e3 d5∓ Zhilin–Timoshenko,   Voronezh 1973.

b) **14 ♘e3** f4 15 ♘f5 ♗×f5 16 ef d5 17 f3 b4∓ Barkan–van der Sterren, World Junior Ch 1975.

12 ...                ♗g7
13 c3

Or 13 000 (13 00 f4!) 13 ... h6 14 ♘b1 00 15 ♘bc3 fe 16 ♗×e4 f5 17 ♘f4! – Gipslis; 13 ... f4!

13 ...                f4

Probably more accurate than:

a) **13 ... h6?!** 14 00 00 15 ♘c2 fe (15 ... f4!? – Sveshnikov, *Informator*) 16 ♗×e4 f5 17 ♘f4!± when Spassky–Sveshnikov, 41st USSR Ch 1973, ended 17 ... ♗d7 18 ♗d5+ ♔h7 19 ♕g6+ ♔h8

20 ♘h5 ♕e7 21 ♘b4 ♘×b4 22 ♗×a8 ♖g8 23 cb 1–0.

b) **13 ... 00!?** when:

b1) **14 g4?!** fg 15 ♘c2 f5 16 ♘de3 f4! 17 ♘×g4 ♔h8 18 ♖g1 ♖b8 19 a3 a5∓ Tseshkovsky – Sveshnikov, Sochi 1974.

b2) **14 ef?!** ♗×d5 15 f6 e4 16 fg ♖e8 17 ♗e2 (17 ♕×d5 ed+ 18 ♔f1 ♘e5∓) 17 ... ♖e5 18 ♕h6 ♖g5! 19 ♖d1 (19 ♘c2!? – Gipslis) 19 ... ♕e7 20 ♘c2 ♖g6 21 ♕f4 ♗×a2! 22 ♘e3 ♕e5∓ (0–1, 60) Tukmakov–Sveshnikov, USSR 1975.

b3) **14 ♘e3** (Gufeld) can be met by 14 ... f4 e.g. 15 ♘f5 ♗×f5 16 ef e4! 17 ♗c2 (17 ♗×e4 ♖e8 18 f3 d5 19 f6 de) 17 ... d5 – AHM.

After 13 ... f4:

B21 14 00

B22 14 g3

**B21**

        **14 00**          00
        15 ♘c2

Or 15 ♖ad1 f5 16 ef ♗×d5 17 f6 ♖×f6 18 ♗×h7+ ♔f8 19 ♖×d5 ♘e7 20 ♕f3 ♖h6 Kuzmin–Vasyukov, USSR 1975.

        15 ...              f5

Or 15 ... ♔h8 16 a4 ba 17 ♖×a4 f5 18 ♖fa1 ♖g8 19 b4 ♗f6 with slower counterplay (but 0–1, 47) Lukin–Timoshenko, 1st game, USSR Cup 1973.

        16 ♘cb4

This is an attempt to improve upon the 3rd Lukin–Timoshenko cup game (1973) which went 16

a4 ♗×d5! 17 ed ♘e7 18 ab e4
19 ♗c4 ab 20 ♗×b5 ♖b8 21 c4
♘×d5 22 ♖a7 ♘c7 23 ♖fa1
♘×d5 24 cd ♕f6∓ and 0–1, 36.

16 ...                 ♘×b4
17 ♘×b4   a5!

This is clearer than 17 ... d5?!
18 ed ♗d7 of Zinn–Sveshnikov,
Dečin 1974.

18 ef               ♗f7
19 ♕h3           ♕d7!
20 ♘c2           d5
21 ♖ad1         ♖a6∓

We don't say that this is best play
for both sides, but the continuation does illustrate many of the
possibilities open to Black: 22
♕g4 ♖h6 23 ♕e2 f3!? (Gufeld
suggested 23 ... b4.) 24 gf ♕e7
25 f4 e4 26 ♗×b5 ♗h5 27 f3
♕c5 28 ♘e3 ef 29 ♕d3 f2+
30 ♔×f2 (30 ♖×f2!? ♗×d1
31 ♘×d1 – Savon) 30 ... ♗×d1
31 ♖×d1 ♔h8! (or 31 ...
♖×h2+∓ – Savon) 32 ♔g2 ♖g8
33 ♘f1 (33 ♔h1 ♖h3 or 33 ♘g4
♗f6 34 h3 ♖h4) 33 ... ♗×c3+
34 ♘g3 ♗×b2 35 ♕×d5
♖×h2+?? (time-trouble, pre-
sumably) 36 ♔×h2 ♕f2+ 37
♕g2 ♕×f4 38 ♕×b2+ 1–0
Klovan – Timoshenko, USSR
Armed Forces Ch, Vilnius 1974;
35 ... ♕e3+ would have given
Black good winning chances.

**B22**

**14 g3**          00(50)

Now we follow Semeniuk–
Timoshenko, USSR Armed
Forces Ch 1975, another very

unclear game that illustrates some
of the possibilities for both sides.

15 000

Gipslis suggested 15 ♖g1!?,
while an earlier game between
the same players in 1975 had
gone 15 gf? ef 16 e5 h6 17 ♖g1
♘×e5! 18 ♕×h6 ♘g6 19 ♕h5
♗×d5 20 ♕×d5 ♖e8+ 21 ♔d2
♕h4 with a strong counter-attack.

15 ...                 f5
16 gf               ♗×d5
17 ed               ♘e7

This looks good for White, but is
practically unanalysable. The
game went on 18 fe ♗×e5 19
♘c2 ♔h8 20 ♘d4 b4 21 ♘e6
♕b6 22 c4 (22 ♘×f8 ♖×f8 is
very risky for White.) 22 ... ♖g8
23 f4 ♗f6 24 c5?! (24 ♗×f5 is
playable.) 24 ... ♕a5 25 ♕f7
♘×d5 26 ♗c4 ♗×b2+ 27
♔×b2 ♖g2+ 28 ♖d2! (despera-
tion, in view of 28 ♔a1 ♕a3 29
♗e2 b3 or 29 ♖d2 ♕c3+) 28 ...
♖×d2+? (Gurvich afterwards
pointed out a saving line for
Black in 28 ... b3! e.g. 29 ♖×g2
♕c3+ 30 ♔b1? ba+ or 30 ♔a3
♕b4+ etc.) 29 ♔a1! 1–0.

**B3**

**11 ef**          ♗×f5(*51*)

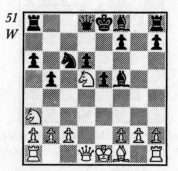

*51*
W

12 ♘d3!?

Others:

a) **12   ♕f3** ♘d4! 13 ♘c7+ ♕×c7 14 ♕×a8+ ♔e7 15 c3 b4! is a promising line for Black, that has occurred in at least two games. Gaprindashvili–Matveyeva, USSR Women's Ch 1973–4, continued 16 cb ♕b6 17 ♗×a6 ♕×b4+ 18 ♔f1 ♕d2 19 h3 ♘d3+ 20 ♗×d3 ♕×d3+ 21 ♔g1 ♗h6! 22 ♕×h8 ♘e2+ (22 ... ♗f4 23 g3! ♕f3 24 ♖e1!=) 23 ♔f1 ♗f4 24 g4! ♘g3+ (24 ... ♕f3! 25 ♖g1 ♗g3∓∓) 25 ♔g1 ♘×h1 26 ♕a8! ♘×f2 27 ♕b7+ ♔f6 28 ♔×f2 ♕e3+ 29 ♔f1 ♕d3+ 30 ♔g1 ½–½.

b) **12 c3** ♗g7 is dangerous;

b1) **13 ♗e2** 00 14 ♘c2 ♗e6 15 00 ♔h8 (15 ... f5!? – Gipslis) 16 ♗f3 (16 f4!? – Gipslis) 16 ... ♖c8 (16 ... f5!? – Gipslis) Sveshnikov–Timoshenko, Moscow 1975.

b2) **13 ♕f3** ♗g6 (13 ... ♗e6 followed by ... 00 and ... f5 is

critical.) 14 h4 e4 15 ♕h3 h5 16 ♘c2 00 17 ♗e2 ♘e5 18 ♘ce3 ♘d3+ 19 ♗×d3 ed 20 00 ♖e8 21 ♖ad1 ♖c8 22 ♘f4± Tal–Shamkovich, Riga 1955.

12 ...          e4

Better than 12 ... ♗e6 (or 12 ... ♗g6 13 h4 e4 14 h5) 13 ♗e4 (±) 13 ... ♗g7 14 ♕h5 ♖c8 15 ♖d1 ♘e7 16 c3 ♖c5 17 ♘×e7 ♕×e7 18 ♘c2 d5 19 ♗f5 ♗×f5 ½–½ Sigurjonsson–Bronstein, Hastings 1975/6.

13 ♕e2

Not 13 ♗×e4 ♗×e4 14 ♕e2 f5 15 f3 ♘d4 16 ♕e3 ♕h4+ Razov–Sivkov, Latvia 1972.

13 ...          ♘d4

Or:

a) **13 ... ♗g7?** 14 ♗×e4 00 15 ♗×f5±± (15 ... ♗×b2 15 ♕g4) Matulović–Ničevski, Yugoslav Ch 1975.

b) **13 ... ♕a5+** 14 c3 b4 is unclear – U.

14 ♕e3          ♗g7
15 ♗×e4          00
16 000 ♗×e4

17 ♕×e4 ♖e8 18 ♕d3? (18 ♕g4 h5! 19 ♕h3 ♖c8∓) 18 ... ♕g5+ 19 ♘e3 ♕f6! 20 c3 ♕×f2 21 cd? (21 ♘ac2 is much better.) 21 ... ♖×e3 22 ♖hf1 ♖c8+   0–1 Nurmi–Chekhov, World Junior Ch 1975 – yet another obscure line!

**C**

9 ...          f5(*52*)

This was apparently first played in Kruglov–Kuzminikh, USSR

1949, with a satisfactory outcome for Black. It also leads to complications of the same order of the previous variations; it is perhaps a matter of taste which one you prefer.

52
W

C1 10 ♗d3
C2 10 ♗c4!?
C3 10 ♘c4
C4 10 ♕h5

or the virtually untested 10 ef ♗×f5 when:

a) **11 ♘d5**= – Zak, in *Sahs* 1971.
b) **11 ♘c4** ♗e6 (11 ... ♘d4 12 ♘e3 ♗e6 13 g3± – Boleslavsky, *The Chess Player* 6) 12 ♘e3 ♗g7 'and Black has counter-chances, in virtue of the threats ... f5 or ... d5' – G.
c) **11 ♗d3** ♗g6 (11 ... ♗e6? 12 ♗e4) 12 ♘c4 f5!? (12 ... d5 13 ♗×g6 dc 14 ♗e4±) 13 ♘d5 b5 or 13 h4 ♘d4; 13 g4!? is worth considering – AHM.

## C1

**10 ♗d3** **♗g7**
10 ... ♕g5 has been tried, unsuccessfully.

11 00 fe
12 ♗×e4 00

13 ♘c4 ♘d4
14 ♗d5 ♗e6∓

Mukhin – Timoshenko, USSR Young Masters' Ch, Cheliabinsk 1974

## C2

**10 ♗c4!?** **♕g5**
Others:

a) **10 ... ♗g7** 11 ♕h5 00 12 ef ♘d4 13 ♗d3± Fischer–Soltis, Manhattan 'Blitz' tournament 1971.
b) **10 ... b5?!** 11 ♗d5 ♗b7 12 ♕h5 ♕e7 13 000± (although Black won) Karakas–Levitina, Women's Interzonal, Menorca 1973.

11 g3 ♗e6
12 ef ♕×f5
13 ♗d3 ♕h3

14 ♗e4 000 15 ♗×c6 bc 16 ♕e2 ♔g7 17 000 (Kirillov–Ilkov, Sofia 1973) is given as ± by M. Possibly Black can play for equalizing simplifications by 17 ... ♗h6+ 18 ♔b1 ♕g4. 10 ♗c4 certainly needs further tests; could it refute 9 ... f5?

## C3

**10 ♘c4** **b5!?**
Or 10 ... f3 11 ♘×e4 ♘d4 12 c3 d5= Bazan–Pelikan, Argentina 1961.

11 ♘e3
Or 11 ... ♗e6 (Timoshenko has also tried 11 ... ♗g7 12 ♗d3 00.) 12 ♗d3 fe 13 ♗×e4 d5 14 ♗f3 ♗g7 15 ♗g4 00 16 ♗×e6 fe 17 ♕g4 ♘d4 18 00 ♕f6 19 ♖ac1 ♖ac8 20 ♘b3 ♖c4∓ (0–1, 37)

Zagorovsky–Timoshenko, Voronezh 1973.

    11 ...        b4
    12 ♘cd5

Geller–Gufeld, Moscow 1970, went 12 ♘b1 fe 13 ♗c4 ♗e6 14 ♗×e6 fe 15 ♕h5+ ♔d7 16 ♘d2 ♕e8 17 ♕h3 ♕g6 18 00 ♗e7 19 a3 with complications.

    12 ...        fe
    13 ♕h5      ♗e6
    14 ♗c4      ♘d4

15 c3 bc 16 bc ♖c8 17 cd ed 18 00 de 10 ♗b3 ♗g7 20 ♖ae1 fe+ 21 ♖×f2 (Savon–Kupreichik, Moscow 1969) 21 ... 00∓ – M.

**C4**

    **10 ♕h5**(*53*)

The most popular reply, but maybe it's an error.

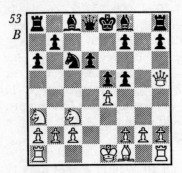

C41 10 ... b5!?
C42 10 ... d5

**C41**

    **10 ...**        **b5!?**

This practically forces White to sacrifice.

    11 ♘a×b5!?

Others:

a) **11 ♘d5** fe.

b) **11 ef** (or 11 000) 11 ... b4 12 ♗c4 (U) 12 ... ♖a7! and what's White's next move? If 13 ♘a×b5 (13 ♗d5? ♘d4) 13 ... ab 14 ♘×b5 ♖b7 – AHM.

    11 ...        ab
    12 ♗×b5      ♗b7

Not 12 ... ♖a6 13 ♗×a6 ♗×a6 14 000 f4 15 g3±± Sokolsky–Tokarev, ¼-final 20th USSR Ch 1952.

    13 ♕×f5

Or:

a) **13 ef** ♕a5! and 14 ... 000 with counter-chances – G.

b) **13 ♗c4!?** ♕f6 14 ♘d5 ♕g6 is unclear; although White won in Tarrasch–Janowski, Vienna 1898 (where the Lasker Variation arose by transposition from 2 ... e6) Larsen said he considered the attack to be unsound.

    13 ...        ♗g7
    14 000      00
    15 ♗×c6      ♗×c6∓

Levchenkov – Sveshnikov, USSR 1969, continued 16 ♖d3 ♗d7! 17 ♕h5 ♗e6 18 ♖hd1 ♗×a2 19 b3 ♗×b3 20 ab ♕a5 21 ♖g3 (better 21 ♖1d2) 21 ... ♖fc8 22 ♔d2 ♖×c3 23 ♖×c3 d5 (0–1, 30).

**C42**

    **10 ...**        **d5**(*54*)

This is a delayed Pelikan, in which White's extra move may prove less useful than Black's.

C421 11 ♘×d5?
C422 11 ed
C423 11 000
C424 11 ♘c4!?

54
W

## C421

**11 ♘×d5?**   ♗×a3
12 ba   ♕a5+
13 c3

Or 13 ♔d1 ♗e6 14 ♘f6+ ♔e7
15 ef ♖d8+ 16 ♗d3 ♕c3 17 ♖c1
♗c4 18 ♘e4 ♖×d3+ !∓∓ Buza–
Ungureanu, Romanian Ch 1973.

13 ...   ♗e6
14 000

Or 14 ♖c1 000 15 ♗c4 ♕c5
16 ♗b3 fe 17 ♘e3 ♘d4! 18 00
♘×b3 19 ab (Schwarz–Virkulov,
Moscow 1972) 19 ... ♕×a3∓ –
M.

14 ...   fe
15 ♘f6+   ♔e7
16 ♘×e4

If 16 ♕h4 ♕×c3+ 17 ♔b1
♗×a2+ !∓∓ – M.

16 ...   ♕×a3+
17 ♔d2   ♖ad8+
18 ♗d3   f5∓∓

19 ♕h4+ ♔d7 20 ♘g5 e4 21
♘×e6 ♔×e6 22 ♕h6+ ♔d7
23 ♗c4 ♕b2+ 24 ♔e3+ ♔c8
25 ♕g7 f4+ ! 26 ♔×f4 ♕×f2+
27 ♔g5 ♕×g2+ 0–1 Kuzmin–
Kupreichik, Minsk 1971.

## C422

**11 ed**   ♗×a3
12 ba   ♕a5
13 ♔d2

Not 13 ♕f3? ♘d4 14 ♕d3
♘b5 15 ♔d2 ♗e6! 16 ♕c4
♘×c3 17 ♕×c3 ♕×d5+ 18
♔c1 00∓∓ Lebedev–Sveshnikov,
Vladimir 1966.

13 ...   ♘e7
14 ♕e2

Meiran – Umansky, USSR
Schoolboys' Ch 1968, went 14
♗c4? ♗e6!! 15 de 000+ 16 ♗d3
♘d5 17 ♕×f5 ♕×c3+ 18 ♔e2
♘f4+ 19 ♔e3 fe 20 ♕e4 ♖d40–1.

14 ...   f6

Others:

a) **14 ... e4** 15 ♕c4 00 16 ♕b4
♕c7 17 ♖d1 ♕e5 18 ♔c1 b5=
Zhelyandinov – Kupreichik,
Vitebsk 1970.

b) **14 ... ♗e6!?** 15 ♕×e5 00 is
unclear – M.

15 ♕c4   ♕×a3
16 ♗e2   ♗d7
17 ♗h5+   ♔d8

18 ♖ab1 b5 19 ♕b3 ♕c5 20
♖hf1 ♖c8∓ Baikov–Zilberstein,
Moscow 1974.

## C423

**11 000**(*55*)

C4231 11 ... ♗×a3!?
C4232 11 ... ♘d4

## C4231

**11 ...**   ♗×a3!?
12 ba   ♘d4

Others:

a) **12 ... fe** 13 ♖×d5 ♕e7 14
♘×e4 ♕×a3+ 15 ♔d1 ♗e6

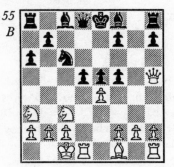

55
B

16 ♘d6+ ♔e7 17 ♕g5+ ♔f8
18 ♕h6+ ♔e7 19 ♕g5+ ½-½
Fischer–Seidler, simul. (Buenos
Aires) 1971.

b) **12 ... ♕a5?** 13 ♘×d5 ♗e6
14 ♘f6+ ♔e7 15 ♗c4! ♘d4 (or
15 ... ♕×a3+ 16 ♔b1 ♕b4+
17 ♗b3 ♔×f6 18 ♖d7! ♗×d7
19 ♕×f7+) 16 ♘d5+ ♔f8?
(16 ... ♗×d5±) 17 ♕h6+ ♔e8
18 ♕f6 ♕×a3+ 19 ♔b1 1-0
Sax–Cox, Norwich 1972.

      13 ef!          ♕a5
      14 ♖×d4!       ed
      15 ♗b5+!       ab
      16 ♖e1+

a) **16 ... ♗e6?** 17 ♖×e6+ ♔d8
18 ♕×f7 ♔c8 19 ♘×d5 ♔b8
20 ♕g7 ♕×a3+ 21 ♔d1 ♖c8
22 ♖b6! ♖a7 23 ♕e5+ 1-0
Luczak – Szczepaniec, Poland
1973.

b) **16 ... ♔d8** (Marić) is not so
clear, e.g. 17 ♕h4+ ♔c7 18
♖e7+ ♔b8.
**C4232**
      **11 ...          ♘d4**
      12 ♘×d5

If 12 ef (seeking transposition
to C4231) Black might try 12 ...

♗×f5 since 13 ♖×d4? ed 14
♕×f5 dc 15 ♕×e5+ fails to 15
... ♕e7 16 ♗b5+ (16 ♕×h8??
♕e1 mate) 16 ... ab 17 ♕×h8
cb+ 18 ♔d2 ♕×a3 etc – AHM
      12 ...          ♗×a3
      13 ba          ♗e6
14 ♕h6?! (14 ♗c4 ♖c8∓) 14 ...
♖c8 15 ♕g7 ♖×c2+ 16 ♔b1
♕b6+!! 17 ♘×b6 ♗×a2+
18 ♔b1 ♘b3 mate; Kalabukhov–
Grigorian, USSR Team Ch 1972
**C424**
      **11 ♘c4!?**
Another unclear line, hardly
tested yet in master play.
      11 ...          ♗b4?!
Others:
a) **11 ... dc?** 12 ♗×c4 ♕c7 (12
... ♕f6 13 ♘d5 ♕d8 14 ♘b6)
13 000 ♘b4 14 ♗b3 (intending
15 a3 and 16 ♘d5)±± – M.
b) **11 ... fe** 12 000 should favour
White.
c) **11 ... d4!** e.g. 12 000 b5!? 13
♘e3 ♗d7 and Black wins a piece
– Botterill and Harding.
      12 000          ♗×c3
Even after 12 ... d4 the complications may still favour White:
13 ef b5!? 14 ♘e4 bc 15 ♗×c4
♕c7! 16 a3! ♗f8 17 ♖he1! ♗b7
... ?
      13 ♖×d5?!
Others:
a3 **13 bc** fe 14 ♘×e4 ♗e6 is
unclear.
b) **13 ed!!** and Black, his king
stuck in the centre, is positionally
lost – Botterill.

13 ...                    ♛f6
14 bc                     ♗e6
15 ♘d6+                   ♔f8
16 ♖c5 fe 17 ♘×b7 ♗c8 18
♖×c6 ♛×c6 19 ♛×e5 f6 20
♛c5+ ♛×c5 21 ♘×c5 f5∓
Murei–Adamson, Sukhumi 1973.
**D**

9 ...                     ♗e6 (*56*)

This is a comparatively staid
line, but it is important as Black's
best line against 8 ♘a3 (see C2
in the next chapter) may transpose into it.

*56*
*W*

10 ♘c4
If 10 ♘d5:
a) **10 ... ♖c8?!** 11 c3! b5 12 ♘c2
♖b8! 13 ♗e2 ♗h6 14 00 00
(Botterill–J. Littlewood, British
Ch 1970) 15 ♘cb4!±.
b) **10 ... f5!** e.g. 11 ♗d3 ♗×d5
12 ed ♘e7 analogously to
Robatsch–Larsen (p. 67).
10 ...                    ♖c8
Not 10 ... b5? (others, see next
chapter) 11 ♘e3 ♗h6 12 ♘cd5
♗×d5 13 ♘×d5 ♘e7 14 a4! b4
15 ♛f3± Honfi–Piket, Wijk aan
Zee 1970.

11 ♘e3
For 11 ♘d5?! ♗×d5 see page
67.
11 ...                    ♘e7!
Not:
a) **11 ... ♗h6** 12 ♘ed5!± –
Sveshnikov.
b) **11 ... ♘d4?!** 12 ♗d3 ♗h6 13
00 00 14 ♘cd5 f5 15 ef ♗×d5
16 ♘ × d5 f6 17 c3 drives out the
knight. Dely–Flesch, Hungarian
Ch 1965, ended 17 ... ♘c6 18
♛h5 ♗g7 19 ♗c4 ♔h8 20 ♖ad1
♘e7 21 ♘e3 ♛b6 22 ♖d2 1–0.
12 ♗d3
Others:
a) **12 ♛f3** ♛b6 (12 ... ♛a5 13
000 is unclear, e.g. 13 ... ♖×c3
14 bc ♛×c3? 15 ♘f5!) 13 000
♗h6 14 ♛×f6 ♗×e3+ 15 fe
♛×e3+ 16 ♔b1 ♖g8 17 ♖×d6
♖×c3 18 bc ♛×c3 19 ♖d3 ½–½
Grabczewski–Markland, Polanica
Zdroj 1973. Now 19 ... ♛e1+
draws by perpetual check, but
possibly there is some way for
Black to get an edge.
b) **12 ♘g4?** (12 ♛h5!? –
Bielczyk) 12 ... ♗g7 13 ♛f3
♛b6! (0–1, 26) Serwinski–
Bielczyk, Poland 1973.
12 ...                    ♛b6
Others:
a) **12 ... ♖c5?** 13 00 h5 14
♘cd5 ♗×d5 15 ♘×d5 ♘×d5
16 ed f5 17 ♗×f5 ♖c4 18 f4!
♖d4 19 ♛e2± Gligorić–N.
Littlewood, Hastings 1963–4.
b) **12 ... ♛d7** 13 ♛f3 ♗g7 14
♘cd5 ♗×d5 15 ed ♛a4 16 00 h5

17 f4 ♖c7 18 h4± Cirić–Eisinger,
Oberhausen 1961.

c) Tal suggested **12 ... ♗h6!?** in
*The Chess Player*, 1975. This may
be quite good, since 13 ♘cd5?
fails to 13 ... ♗×d5 14 ♘×d5
♘×d5 15 ed ♕a5+.

13 00                 ♕×b2

Following Larsen's analysis in
*Skakbladet*, 1973.

14 ♘cd5        ♗×d5
15 ♘×d5(*57*)

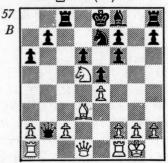

57
B

Or 15 ed ♕d4 16 ♕f3 when:

a) **16 ... ♗g7?** 17 ♖ab1 ♖c7 18
♗×a6! ba 19 ♖b8+ ♘c8 20
♘f5 ♕a7 21 ♘×g7+ ♔f8 22
♖×c8+ ♖×c8 23 ♕×d6±±.

b) **16 ... ♕f4!** and now:

b1) **17 ♕×f4?** ef 18 ♘f5! ♘×d5
19 ♗e4 ♖c5!∓.

b2) **17 ♕h3:**

b21) **17 ... e4?!** 18 g3 ♖g8! (18
... ♕f3? 19 ♘c4±± Lombardy–
Markland, Nice Olympiad 1974)
19 ♕×h7 ed! offers Black some
chances.

b22) **17 ... ♕h6** 18 ♕f3 ♕f4
obliges White to retreat his queen
or take a draw.

15 ...                ♘×d5

16 ed

'Afterwards, Brinck–Claussen
said that if he had realized how
many chances White had in this
position, he would not have had
the courage to take the b-pawn' –
Larsen. Is Black really in much
danger?

Bely    v.    Brinck–Claussen,
Hastings 1963–4, continued 16 ...
♕d4 17 ♕f3 (17 ♖b1!?) 17 ...
♔e7 18 ♖ab1 ♖c7 19 ♖b3 ♗h6
20 ♖fb1 20 ... b5 21 ♖b4 ♕c5
(More active than 21 ... ♕a7 of
Liberzon–Gerusel, Solingen 1974)
22 a4 ♗d2 23 ♖h4 ♗g5 24 ♖g4
(24 ♖h5!? ba 25 h4 is another
unclear winning try.) 24 ... h5 25
♖e4 ♕×d5 26 ab ab 27 h4 ♗d2
28 ♖×b5 ♕a8 29 ♕e2 ♗c3 and
Black stood soundly (0–1, 49).

Conclusion

Pelikan's 9 ... d5 often gets
results, but can Black hold his
own in one or other of A1 or A2
with the ideas we suggest? 9 ... b5
10 ♘d5 f5 is only for the brave
as White has three dangerous
plans in reply: 11 ♗×b5, 11
♗d3 (the B22 variant) and 11 ef
♗×f5 (and either 12 c3 or 12
♗d3). 9 ... f5 looks better, but
again very obscure; the critical
replies are 10 ♗c4 and 10 ef
♗×f5 11 ♗d3. 9 ... ♗e6 is more
positional; in line D Tal's 12 ...
♗h6 may be an improvement
upon Larsen's barely playable 12
... ♕b6.

# 6  5 ... e5, 8 ♘a3

After 1 e4 c5 2 ♘f3 ♘c6 3 d4 cd 4 ♘×d4 ♘f6 5 ♘c3 e5 6 ♘db5 d6 7 ♗g5 a6 8 ♘a3(*58*) the Lasker Variation faces perhaps its severest test. White retains his bishop for the time being, and does not allow Black the mobile f-pawn which so often in the previous chapter was able to undermine White's grip on the central squares. In this context it is worth quoting the opinion of R (1957): 'Black is forced to develop his position in a normal way. But it is precisely this normal development of his forces that gives Black all sorts of trouble ... The move 8 ♘a3! is therefore undoubtedly the Achilles' heel of the modern Argentinian way of playing Lasker's old attack'. Nevertheless, we shall see, Black can get all sorts of chances, and in fact 8 ♘a3 is less often played than 8 ♗×f6 by masters nowadays.

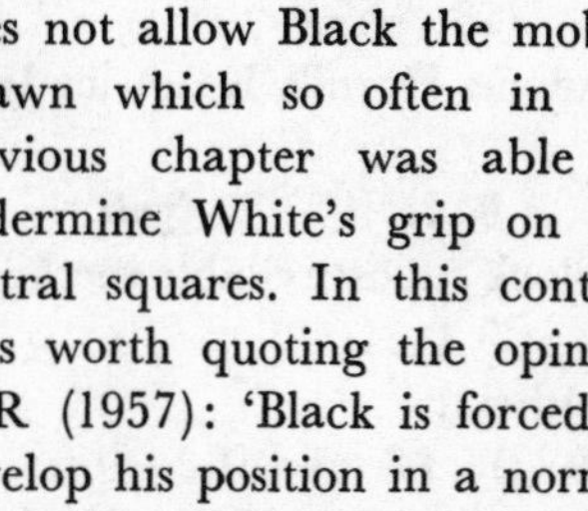

A 8 ... d5?!
B 8 ... ♗e7
C 8 ... ♗e6
D 8 ... b5!?

## A

**8 ...　　　　d5?!**

Pelikan's idea is less satisfactory here, as White has two bishops.

9 ♘×d5　　♗×a3
10 ba　　　♕a5+
11 ♕d2

Bivshev – Klaman, Leningrad ½-final, 24th USSR Ch 1956, went 11 ♗d2 ♕d8 12 ♘×f6+ ♕×f6 13 ♗d3 00 14 00 ♕e7 (14 ... ♗e6 15 ♗c3 ♕e7± – U) 15 ♕c1 ♗e6 16 ♕b2 ♖fd8 with possibly an edge to White (but ½–½, 46).

11 ...　　　　♕×d2+
12 ♗×d2　　♘×d5
13 ed　　　　♘d4

a) **14 ♗d3±** Darga–Kinzel,

58
B

Berne 1957; White has a useful bishop pair.

b) **14  000** (Stoyanov–Milkov, Bulgarian Corres Ch 1972–3) is not so good.

**B**

**8 ...                    ♗e7**

This is not active enough.

9 ♘c4                    ♗e6

Or:

a) **9 ... 00** 10 ♗×f6 ♗×f6 11 ♕×d6 ♗e6 12 000 ♗g5+ 13 ♔b1 ♕f6 14 ♕c5 ♘d4 15 ♕×e5 ♕×e5 16 ♘×e5± Estrin–Goldenov, USSR 1956.

b) **9 ... ♘d4?!** when:

b1) **10 ♘e3** ♗e6 11 ♗d3 00 12 00 b5 13 ♗×f6 ♗×f6 14 ♘cd5 ♗g5± Vogt–Schöneberg, E. German Ch 1972.

b2) **10 ♗×f6** and now:

b21) **10 ... gf** 11 ♘d5 f5 12 c3 ♘b5 13 ♘cb6± Kopilov–Kuzminikh, USSR 1951.

b22) **10 ... ♗×f6** 11 ♘d5 b5 12 ♘cb6 ♖b8 13 ♘×c8 ♖×c8 14 c3 ♘c6 15 a4! (B) 15 ... ♖b8 16 ab ab 17 ♖a6! ♕c8 18 ♗×b5! ♖×b5 19 ♕a4 ♖×b2 20 ♖a8±± Armas–Horvath, Hungary 1973.

10 ♗×f6! gf
11 ♘e3
Or 11 ♘d5!? (11 ♗d3 ♘d4 12 ♘e3 below) when:

a) **11 ... ♗×d5** 12 ed ♘d4 13 c3 ♘f5 14 ♕g4± Alexander–Wood, England 1956.

b) **11 ... f5** 12 ef ♗×f5 13 c3 ♗e6 14 a4 ♘a5 15 ♘cb6 ♗×d5 16 ♘×d5 ♖c8 17 b4 ♘c4 18 a5

♗g5 19 ♖a2! ♗h6 20 ♕g4± Walther – Lindblom, Moscow 1956.

11 ...                    ♘d4
Or 11 ... ♕d7 12 ♘cd5 ♗d8 13 ♕h5± Blau–Plater, Hilversum 1947.

12 ♗d3
12 ♗c4 is less clear, e.g. 12 ... ♖c8 13 ♗d5 ♕b6 14 ♖b1 00 15 00 ♔h8! 16 ♔h1 f5 with a sharp game; Karpov–Spurgeon, London simul 1972.

12 ...                    ♕d7
13 ♘cd5                    ♗d8
14 c3                    ♘c6
15 ♕h5±
Vladone–Hurnik, Katowice 1970.

**C**

**8 ...                    ♗e6**

Black's most reliable method

9 ♘c4 (59)

Others:

a) **9 ♗×f6** ♕×f6? (9 ... gf, chapter 6) 10 ♘d5 ♗×d5 (10 ... ♕d8? 11 ♘c4) 11 ed ♘b8 12 ♕g4 ♘d7 13 ♗d3 g6 14 00 ♕e7 15 ♕g4 ♘c5 16 ♘c4± Möhring–Weber, E. German Ch 1963.

59
B

b) **9 ♘d5?** ♗×d5? 10 ♗×f6?
(10 ♕×d5 ♘×d5 11 ♗×d8
♘e3!∓) 10 ... ♕a5+ 11 c3
♗×e4 12 ♘c4 ♕c7 (0–1, 43)
Sellman–Bird, London 1883.

C1 9 ... ♘d4

C2 9 ... ♖c8!

a) **9 ... h6?** 10 ♗×f6 ♕×f6 11
♘b6 ♖b8 12 ♘cd5 ♕b6 13 ♕d3
♗×d5 14 ♘×d5 ♗e7 15 g3
♗d8 16 000 b5 17 f4± Ribli–
Zinn, Zalaegerszeg 1969.

b) **9 ... b5** 10 ♗×f6 ♕×f6 (10
... gf± chapter 6) 11 ♘e3 ♕d8
12 ♘cd5 g6 13 a4 b4 14 ♗c4
♗h6 15 ♕d3 00 16 ♗×a6 f5 17
♗b7 and White soon won
material; Bednarski – Kavalek,
Krakow 1964.

**C1**

**9 ...                 ♘d4**

10 ♗×f6!

Others:

a) **10 ♘d5** ♗×d5 11 ed when:

a1) **11 ... ♗e7?** 12 c3 ♘b5 13
♗e3!± Lukin–Kupreichik, USSR
Spartakiad 1967.

a2) **11 ... b5** 12 ♘e3 ♕a5+ 13
c3 ♘e4 14 ♗h4 g5 15 ♗g3
♘×c3 16 ♕d2 b4 with com-
plications – B. A possible continuation is 17 ♘c4 (17 bc? bc
18 ♕d3 ♖b8!) 17 ... ♕×d5 18
bc with about equal chances.
Black has only two pawns for
the piece, but they give him a
massive centre.

b) **10 ♘e3** when:

b1) **10 ... ♖c8!?** 11 ♗d3 ♗e7
12 ♗×f6 ♗×f6 13 00 00 14

♘cd5 ♗g5 15 c3 ♘c6 16 ♕e2
♘e7 (Karaklajić–Pilnik, Moscow 1956) 17 ♗c4±.

b2) **10 ... ♗e7** 11 ♗×f6 ♗×f6
12 ♘cd5 ♗g5 13 c3 ♗×e3!? 14
♘×e3 ♘c6 15 ♗c4 00 16 00
♕c7 17 ♕d3 ♘e7± Kavalek–
Benko, Caracas 1970.

10 ...                 ♕×f6

Not 10 ... gf 11 ♘e3 which is a
classic case of the Lasker Variation failing. Suetin, in *Modern
Chess Opening Theory*, gives this
position as an example of how an
organic weakness in the opponent's camp can facilitate the long-
term positioning of your pieces.
Bronstein–Pilnik, Moscow 1956,
continued 11 ... ♖c8 12 ♗d3 h5
13 00 h4 14 ♘cd5 ♗g7 15 c3
♘c6 16 ♕f3 ♖h6 17 ♘f5±±.

11 ♘b6!

Veresov's suggestion.

Less effective are:

a) **11 ♘e3** when Black could try
11 ... g6!? (MCO) or 11 ... ♗e7
12 ♗d3 00 13 00± – Euwe.

b) **11 ♗d3** ♕d8! (11 ... ♕g6 12
00 ♗e7 13 ♘e3± – P) 12 00 ♗e7
13 ♘e3 00 14 ♘cd5 ♗g5
(unclear – B) 15 c3 ♘c6, intending ... ♘e7= – U.

11 ...                 ♖b8

Or 11 ... ♖d8 12 ♘bd5!
♗×d5 13 ♘×d5 ♕g6±.

12 ♘cd5                 ♕d8

13 c3

Clearly this is a disastrous
position for Black.

a) **13 ... ♗×d5** 14 ♘×d5 ♘e6

15 g3 ♗e7 16 a4 00 17 ♗h3 ♖e8
18 00 ♗c8 19 a5 ♘g5 20 ♗f5
g6? 21 ♗d7!±± Tal–Wade,
Reykjavik 1964.

b) **13 ... ♘c6** 14 ♕a4! ♗e7? (14
... ♗×d5 15 ♘×d5±) 15 ♗a×6!
♗×d5 16 ♘×d5 ♖a8 17 ♕b5
♖×a6 18 ♕×b7±± – B.

**C2**

**9 ...              ♖c8!**(60)

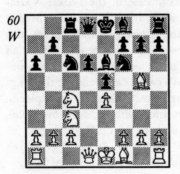

60
W

C21 10 ♘e3
C22 10 ♘d5

a) **10 ♗×f6** gf is a common
transposition to chapter 6, D.

b) **10 ♗d3!?** when:

b1) **10 ... ♘b4** 11 ♘e3 ♕b6 12
♗×f6 ♘×d3+ 13 cd gf 14
♘cd5 ♕d8 15 ♕f3 ♗e7 16 00
♗×d5 17 ♘×d5 ♖g8 18 ♖ac1±
Fuchs–Svedenborg, Tel Aviv
Olympiad 1964.

b2) **10 ... ♗e7!** (e.g. 11 ♗×f6
♗×f6 12 ♘e3 ♗g5 etc.) offers
sufficient counterplay – AHM.

**C21**

**10 ♘e3              ♗e7**

10 ... h6 wastes a tempo, e.g.
11 ♗×f6 ♕×f6 12 ♗e2 ♕d8

13 ♗g4 ♘d4 14 ♗×e6 ♘×e6
15 00 ♗e7± Janošević–Puc,
Yugoslav Ch 1949.

11 ♗×f6

Or 11 ♗c4 00 12 00 ♘d4 13
♗×f6 ♗×f6 14 ♗d5 b5 15 ♘e2
♕c7 16 c3± Ardiansjah–R.
Jamieson, Nice Olympiad 1974.

11 ...              ♗×f6
12 ♘cd5!              ♗g5
13 c3!

Minev's recommendation.

Others:

a) The puzzling game Westerinen–
Johansson, Halle 1963, continued
**13 ♘f5?!** ♗×f5 14 ef ♘d4 15 c3
♕a5!∓.

b) **13 ♗e2** ♘d4!= – Gheorghiu.

13 ...              00
14 g3              g6
15 h4              ♗×e3
16 ♘×e3

Georgescu–Vaisman, Romanian
Ch 1973; the position is unclear.
Gheorghiu now suggested 16 ...
b5 in *Chess Player* 6. Evidently line
C21 needs further tests.

**C22**

**10 ♘d5              ♗×d5**
11 ♗×f6

Or 11 ed when:

a) **11 ... ♘b8** 12 ♗e2 ♗e7 13 00
00 14 a4 ♘bd7 15 ♗e3 ♘e8 16 f3
f5 17 b4 ♘ef6 18 ♘a5 ♕c7 19
c4 ♕b8 20 ♖c1 ♗d8= Sokolov–
Trifunović, Yugoslav Ch 1956.

b) **11 ... ♘e7** 12 ♕d3!? (12
♗×f6 below) 12 ... ♘e×d5 (12
... ♘f×d5?? 13 ♗×e7) 13 000
and now:

b1) **13 ...** ♗**e7** 14 ♗×f6 ♘×f6
15 ♘×d6+ ♛×d6 16 ♛×d6
♗×d6 17 ♖×d6± Tal–Jordan,
telex simul Tal v. Australia 1974.
b2) **13 ... b5!?** (or 13 ... ♛c7 14
c3=) 14 ♗×f6 ♛×f6 15
♛×d5? (15 ♘×d6+ =) 15 ...
bc 16 ♗×c4?? ♛f4+ ∓∓ – Tal.

11 ...          gf(*61*)

Or 11 ... ♛×f6!? 12 ♛×d5
♗e7= – Tal in *Chess Player* 6.

61
W

12 ed!?

Larsen, in his *Selected Games of
Chess*, wrote: 'After this I prefer
the black position!'

He gave as superior 12 ♛×d5
with this analysis:

a) **12 ...** ♘**d4?** 13 000 ♛e7 14
♖×d4 giving White more than
enough for the exchange;

b) **12 ...** ♘**b4** 13 ♛d2 d5! 14 ed
and now:

b1) **14 ...** ♛×**d5** 'with a rather
even game'.

b2) 'or perhaps **14 ...** ♘×**c2+!?**
15 ♛×c2 ♗b4+ followed by ...
b5'. Bhend–Svedenborg, Lugano
Olympiad 1968, in fact continued
16 ♔d1 b5 17 ♛e4 bc 18 ♗×c4

♛b6 19 ♔e2 ♗d6 20 ♗b3
♔e7=. Black has good chances
for the pawn, but the presence
of opposite coloured bishops
makes a win very difficult.

12 ...          ♘e7
13 ♗d3

Others:

a) **13 b4!?** when:

a1) **13 ...** ♛**c7?** 14 a4 b5 15 ab
ab 16 ♘×d6+!± Gligorić v.
Brink–Claussen, Hastings 1963–
4.

a2) **13 ... f5!** with a good game –
Larsen.

b) **13** ♛**f3** f5 14 ♛a3 ♖c5!∓ –
U.

c) **13** ♗**e2!?** f5 14 ♛d2 b5! with
nasty threats – AHM.

13 ...          f5
14 00          ♗g7
15 ♛h5          e4

16 ♗e2 00 17 c3!? f4! 18 ♛g5
b5 19 ♘d2 f5 20 a4 ♔h8! 21
♘b3 (21 ab f3! or 21 f3 ♗f6! –
Larsen) 21 ... f3 22 gf ♗×c3!
23 ♔h1 ♗×b2 24 ♖a2 ♗e5 25
ab ♖g8 26 ♛h5 (26 ♛h4 ♛f8)
26 ... ♘×d5 27 ba ♘f4 28
♛×f5 ♛h4 29 ♗d1 ♘e2 30
♛×e5+ de 31 ♖×e2 and 0–1
(31 ... ♛h3!) Robatsch–Larsen,
Halle 1963.

**D**

8 ...          **b5!?**(*62*)

A move revived by Timoshenko
and other players from Chely-
abinsk. Although Black may be
on thin ice, this is a fighting
alternative to C2, and should be

studied in conjunction with line B in chapter 5.

62
W

9 ♘d5

9 ♗×f6 must be met by 9 ... gf (chapter 5).

Instead 9 ... ♕×f6 10 ♘d5 ♕d8 probably favours White:
a) **11 c3** ♘e7 12 ♘c2 ♘×d5 13 ♕×d5 ♗e6 14 ♕d2 ♗e7 15 a4 00 16 ♗d3 d5 17 ed (Krnic–Radojević, Sombor 1970) 17 ... ♗×d5! 18 ♘e3 ♗c6= – M.
b) **11 c4** when:
b1) **11 ... b4?** 12 ♕a4 ♗d7 13 ♘b5 (13 ... ab 14 ♕×a8!)±± Lerner–Tseitlin, USSR Armed Forces Ch 1973.
b2) **11 ... ♘e7** (Adorjan–Sveshnikov, Budapest 1967) 12 cb ♘×d5 13 ♕×d5 (or 13 ed!± – U) 13 ... ♗e6 14 ♕d2 d5 15 ba ♗×a3 16 ♗b5+! – Sveshnikov.
c) **11 ♗×b5!?** (Boleslavsky in *Chess Player*) is unclear after 11 ... ab 12 ♘a×b5 ♖a7 – compare chapter 5, B1.

After 9 ♘d5:
D1 9 ... ♗e6?!
D2 9 ... ♕a5+
D3 9 ... ♗e7

**D1**

9 ...          ♗e6?!
10 c4!          b4

Or 10 ... ♗×d5 11 ed ♘d4 12 cb ab?! 13 ♗×b5+ ♔e7 (Weisman–Burger, New York 1953) 14 ♗c4± – M.

11 ♗×f6          gf
12 ♘c2?!

White should play 12 ♕a4, as in note b1 to White's 9th. A possible continuation is 12 ... ♗d7 13 ♘b5! ab 14 ♕×a8 ♕×a8 15 ♘c7+ ♔e7 16 ♘×a8 ♘d4 with some play for the exchange, but perhaps not enough after 17 ♖d1 ♗h6 18 ♘d5 – AHM.

After 12 ♘c2 Black has excellent fighting chances. Runau–Markland, Hastings Challengers 1969–70, continued 12 ... ♖b8 13 ♗e2 ♗e7 14 ♗g4? ♕d7 15 ♗×e6 fe 16 ♕h5+ ♔d8 17 ♘de3 b3 18 ab ♖×b3 19 00 ♖×b2 20 c5 dc 21 ♖fd1 ♘d4 22 ♖×a6 ♕b7 23 ♖aa1 ♔d7 24 f4 ♖a8 25 ♖×a8 ♕×a8 26 ♕×h7? ♕a2 27 fe fe 28 ♘e1 ♖d2 29 ♘d3 ♖×d3! 30 ♖×d3 ♕e2 31 ♖×d4+ ed 32 ♘f1 c4 33 ♕g7 ♕×e4 34 ♕g3 c3 35 ♕f2 c2 36 ♕d2 d3 37 ♕c3 e5 0–1.

**D2**

9 ...          ♕a5+
10 ♗d2

Not 10 ♕d2?! ♕×d2+ 11 ♔×d2? (11 ♗×d2 ♘×d5 12 ed ♘e7=) 11 ... ♘×e4+ 12 ♔e3

♘ × g5 13 ♘c7+ ♔d8 14 ♘ × a8 d5!∓ – U.

10 ...            ♛d8
11 ♘ × f6+

Others:

a) **11 ♗d3** (Gulko–Goldin, Moscow Ch 1974) 11 ... ♗e6! e.g. 12 c4 bc 13 ♛a4 ♗ × d5? (13 ... ♗d7 is alright for Black.) 14 ed cd 15 dc! ♛c7 16 ♘b5± – AHM.

b) **11 c4!?** (Müller) 11 ... ♘ × e4?! (possibly 11 ... b4!? or 11 ... ♘ × d5 and 12 ... ♘d4) 12 cb ♘e7 13 ♗e3 ♖b8 14 ♗c4 ♛a5+ 15 b4 ♛ × a3 16 ♗c1 ♘c3 17 ♛d2 ♛a4 18 ♗b3 ♘ed5 19 ♗ × a4 ♘ × a4 20 ♛ × d5±± Mikhailchishin – Timoshenko, USSR Cup 1973.

11 ...            ♛ × f6
12 c4

12 ♗d3 is also crucial:

a) **12 ... ♛b6?!** 13 00± e.g. 13 ... ♗h3? 14 ♛f3 ♗e6 15 c3 h5 16 ♘c2 ♗e7 17 ♛e2 h4 18 a4!± Jansa–Radojević, Sombor 1970.

b) **12 ... ♗e6** 13 c3 (13 c4!? – AHM) 13 ... ♛d8! meeting 14 ♘c2 by 14 ... d5= – M.

12 ...            ♛g6

Or:

a) **12 ... bc?** 13 ♘ × c4 ♛g6 (Begun–Hotiashov, USSR 1974) 14 ♛a4! ♗d7 15 ♘b6 ♘b8 16 ♘ × d7 ♘ × d7 17 ♖c1±± – Boleslavsky in *Chess Player* 7.

b) **12 ... b4** 13 ♘c2 ♛g6 14 ♛f3 ♖b8 should be playable, although Black lost in Sorokin–Korchnoi, Leningrad 1950.

13 f3            ♗e7(63)

63
W

Black has excellent practical chances, e.g.:

a) **14 ♗e3** ♘d4 is unclear – Parma.

b) **14 g3** 00 15 cb ♘d4 16 ♗e3 (Minić–Radojević, Sombor 1964) 16 ... f5! – M.

c) **14 ♔f2!?** 00! 15 cb ♘d4 16 ♗e3 f5 17 ♗ × d4 fe! 18 ♗e3 ♗h4+ 19 ♔e2 (Kurajica–Radojević, Sombor 1968) 19 ... ♗b7! with complications – M.

d) **14 cb!?** ♗h4+ 15 g3 ♗ × g3+ 16 hg ♛ × g3+ 17 ♔e2 ♘d4+ 18 ♔e3 f5 19 ♗c3 fe 20 ♗ × d4 ed+ 21 ♛ × d4 ♛ × f3+ 22 ♔d2 ♛ × h1 23 ♛ × g7 (Radulov–Cobo, Havana 1969) 23 ... ♛h2+ 24 ♗e2 ♛e5∓ – Parma.

These lines tend to show that Black need not fear plans based on the advance c4, because in most cases he can sacrifice his Q-side pawns if necessary (compare the Benko Gambit!). Plans involving c3, ♘c2 and an eventual a4 are positionally more dangerous, in general.

**D3**

9 ...                    ♗e7(64)

64
W

D31 10 ♘×e7
D32 10 ♗×f6

10 c3 ♗e6 (Why not 10 ...
♘×d5! 11 ed ♗×g5 etc.?)
11 ♗×f6 see D32.

**D31**

10 ♘×e7    ♕×e7

10 ... ♘×e7 11 ♗×f6 gf 12 c4
♗b7 is quite interesting, e.g. 13
cb ♗×e4 14 ♕a4 d5 15 ba+
♔f8 (0–1, 45) Semeniuk–
Sveshnikov, ½-final USSR Armed
Forces Ch 1975. Note again the
similarities to the Benko Gambit!

11 c3

11 c4 is critical, e.g. 11 ... ♘d4
(11 ... b4!?; 11 ... ♗b7!?) 12 cb
(12 ♘c2!±) 12 ... ♕b7 13 f3
♘×e4 14 fe ♕×e4+ with an
unclear position – Sveshnikov,
*Informator* 16.

11 ...          h6

Or 11 ... ♗b7:

a) 12 ♗d3 h6 13 ♗h4 00 14 00
♖ad8 15 c4 bc 16 ♗×c4 g5 17
♗g3 ♘×e4 (0–1, 25) Milosev–
Joksić, Vrsac 1973.

b) 12 ♘c2 h6 13 ♗×f6 ♕×f6
14 a4 00! 15 ♘e3 b4∓ –
Sveshnikov.

12 ♗×f6

Or 12 ♗h4 00 when:

a) 13 ♕f3 g5 14 ♗g3 d5 15 ed
♗g4 16 ♕d3 ♖ad8∓ – Timo-
shenko.

b) 13 ♘c2 g5 14 ♗g3 ♘×e4 15
♕d5 ♘×g3 16 hg ♗b7 17 ♕d2
(17 ♖×h6? ♘d4) 17 ... ♕e6∓
Kotkov – Timoshenko, USSR
1967.

12 ...          ♕×f6
13 ♘c2

13 ♗e2 00 (Jahr–Timoshenko,
Hastings Challengers 1966–7) was
no better.

13 ...          00
14 g3          ♖b8
15 b4          ♗b7

16 ♗g2 ♘e7 17 00 ♕g6 18 ♘e3
♖fd8∓ Minić–Gligorić, Yugoslav Ch 1959.

**D32**

10 ♗×f6    ♗×f6(65)

65
W

11 c3

Others:

a) 11 ♗d3 ♗g5 12 00 00 13 c4 b4

14 ♘c2 a5 15 a3 b3 16 ♘ce3 ♗×e3 17 fe a4 18 ♕h5 ♗e6∓ Jakovljevski–Sveshnikov, Yugoslavia v. USSR 1969.

b) 11 **♗e2** 00 12 00 **♗g5** 13 c3 (Jansa–Jongsma, Budva 1963) 13 ... ♘e7 14 ♘c2 ♘×d5 15 ♕×d5 ♗e6 16 ♕d3 d5∓ – Sveshnikov.

11 ...          00

This may be premature.

Others:

a) 11 ... **♗e6**

a1) **12** ♘×**f6+** gf 13 ♘c2 00 14 ♗d3 ♔h8 15 00 ♖g8 16 ♘e3 b4!= Olafsson–Larsen, Zürich 1959.

a2) **12 ♗e2** (or 12 ♘c2 and 13 a4 – Euwe) 12 ... ♗g5 13 ♘c2 f5 14 a4 ♖b8 15 ab ab 16 ef ♗×f5 17 ♘cb4!± Estrin–Romanov, USSR 1956.

b) **11 ...  ♗g5** 12 ♘c2 ♖b8 deserves attention:

b1) **13 ♗d3** 00 14 00 ♗e6 15 a4 ba 16 ♘db4 ♘e7 17 ♗×a6 ♗b3 18 ♕e2 ♕c7 19 ♗d3 ♖bd8 20 ♘a3 d5 (½-½, 43) Horvat–Panchenko, USSR pioneers' tourney 1970.

b2) **13 a4!?** and if 13 ... ba 14 ♘cb4 – AHM.

12 ♘c2          ♗g5

Sveshnikov suggested 12 ... ♖b8!? first. This was tried in Kapengut–Goldin, Baltic Team Ch 1974: 13 ♕f3!? ♗g5 14 h4 ♗h6 15 g4 f6 16 ♖d1 ♗e6 17 ♕g2 ♖b7 18 ♗e2 g6 19 ♖h3 ♘e7 (19 ... ♗×d5 20 ♖×d5 ♘e7 21 ♖d1 ♗f4 22 ♖3d3 –

Kapengut) 20 ♘cb4! ♘×d5 21 ed ♗c8 22 ♘×a6 f5 23 g5 ♗g7 24 ♘b4. Now, instead of 24 ... e4? 25 f4!, Black could have tried 24 ... f4! 25 ♗g4 e4 as suggested by Boleslavsky.

13 a4!

Others:

a) **13 h4?!** ♗h6 14 ♘ce3 ♗×e3 15 ♘×e3 ♘e7 16 ♗e2 ♗e6 17 ♗f3 ♕b6 18 ♕d2 ♖ab8 19 00 b4 20 c4 ♘c6 21 b3 ♘d4 22 ♗e2 f5∓ Hoogendoorn–Timoshenko, Hastings Challengers 1966–7.

b) **13 ♘ce3** when:

b1) **13 ... ♗×e3** (probably premature) 14 ♘×e3 ♗h6 15 ♗e2 ♘e7 = – U.

b2) **13 ... ♗e6** 14 ♗e2 ♖b8 15 00 a5 16 g3 ♕d7 17 ♔h1 ♗×e3 18 ♘×e3 ♘e7 19 ♗f3 b4 20 c4 f5= (0–1, 40) Muir–Chekhov, World Junior Ch 1975.

13 ...          ba

Against Kupreichik, earlier in 1973, Sveshnikov played 13 ... ♖b8±.

14 ♖×a4          a5
15 ♗c4

Estrin – Kimelfeld, Moscow 1967, went 15 b4!? ♗e6 16 b5 ♘b8 17 ♗e2 ♘d7 18 ♖a2 ♘c5 with complications.

After 15 ♗c4:

a) **15 ...  ♖b8?** (Karpov–Sveshnikov, 41st USSR Ch 1973) 16 ♕a1!±.

b) **15 ... ♗d7** (intending ... ♕b8 and ... ♗d8–b6) awaits a test – Sveshnikov.

Conclusion

The safest line for Black is 8 ... ♗e6, normally transposing to D of chapter 5, although the new line 10 ♘e3 may give White some advantage.

The line most in the spirit of the Lasker Variation is 8 ... b5 (in conjunction with B of chapter 5). This is what international master Sveshnikov and the other young Russians play. They may even have some secrets we haven't discovered, so home analysis here could prove most worthwhile!

# 7 Boleslavsky: Introduction

The variation rightly named after the Soviet grandmaster Isaac Boleslavsky arises by:

| | |
|---|---|
| 1 e4 | c5 |
| 2 ♘f3 | ♘c6 |
| 3 d4 | cd |
| 4 ♘×d4 | ♘f6 |
| 5 ♘c3 | d6 |
| 6 ♗e2 | e5 (66) |

The main strategic ideas behind this move have already been discussed in the introduction. Black establishes a bulwark in the centre with the gain of a tempo, taking advantage of the fact that White's sixth move does not fight directly for control of the key square d5. A second detail is that, ... d6 having already been played, Black does not fear the reply ♘db5 which only loses White some time. These factors mean that Black has from the start a more solid position than in the La Bourdonnais and Lasker variations. White too is about to put his king into relative safety by K-side castling. So we may expect a more placid and positional game to arise from the Boleslavsky than from the lines discussed so far.

Nevertheless a tense struggle is likely to develop, so that although combinations and sacrifices are uncommon there are plenty of chances for both sides to get an advantage. Black will usually try to attack the white Q-side pawns, or to undermine the centre with ... d5, while White may either try to open the game by f4, or to strangle Black by piece control of d5. Although there are still some relatively unexplored alleys, the overall impression is that Black cannot be prevented from obtaining a good position if he plays correctly.

Because the Boleslavsky has this good reputation, masters in the 1960s and 1970s have tended to avoid it, playing not 6 ♗e2 but 6 ♗c4 (Sozin), 6 ♗g5 (Richter–Rauzer) or one of the moves discussed in the next chapter. Also Black has not always employed the Boleslavsky when given the opportunity, since 6 ... g6 (Dragon) and 6 ... e6 (Scheveningen) are also good moves, but it is arguable that 6 ... e5 is the move which gives a positional player his best winning chances. Fashions in chess openings fluctuate, and it may not be long before the Boleslavsky is in regular use again, refurbished with new plans for White and Black. In the meantime, the reader will note that the majority of examples are taken from its 1950s heyday; there are perhaps not many people left who know the variation well so even some of the old lines may have surprise value.

66
W

From the diagram:

**7 ♘f3** – chapter 8

**7 ♘b3** – chapter 9

**7 ♘f5?** ♗×f5 (or 7 ... d5 – Panov and Estrin) 8 ef d5! 'and Black has quickly solved his opening problems' – Suetin.

**7 ♘db5!?** a6 8 ♘a3 is a form of Lasker Variation, in which White has practically lost a tempo since his ♗e2 is not playing a very active role. E. Pedersen–Larsen, Danish Ch 1964, continued 8 ...

♗e6 (8 ... b5!?) 9 ♗g5 (9 ♘c4 b5 10 ♘e3 ♘d4∓ – S) 9 ... ♖c8 (compare p. 66) 10 ♘c4 ♘d4 11 ♘d5 ♗×d5 12 ed ♕c7 13 ♘e3 ♘×c2+ 14 ♘×c2 ♕×c2 15 ♗×f6 ♕×d1+ and Black eventually won with his extra pawn.

This only leaves:

**7 ♘×c6**

a move which, despite its bad reputation, is perhaps no worse than the regular retreats. By comparison with the line 4 ... e5 5 ♘×c6?!, for example, Black has already played ... d6, so that his king's bishop cannot come directly out to b4 or c5, and the subsequent thematic advance ... d5 will cost him a tempo – and it will, moreover, be harder to effect. On the other hand, Black has no immediate worries about the weakness of d5 and can instead switch to a plan based on piece play, using e5 as a post for his knight if White plays f4 (as he must, sooner or later, in order to get active play).

**7 ...** bc

**8 00**

Or:

a) **8 ♕d3!?** when:

a1) **8 ... d5?** 9 ed cd 10 ♕g3±.

a2) **8 ... ♗e7** 9 00 see B, below.

b) **8 f4?!** when:

b1) **8 ... ♕b6?!** 9 ♕d3 ♗e7 10 ♗e3 ♕×b2? 11 ♖b1 ♕a3 12 00 ♘d7 13 ♕c4± – S.

b2) **8 ... ♘d7!** and not 9 f5? ♕b6! – Barden.

8 ...                    ♗e7 (67)

This move is invariably played but Barden, in *A Guide to Chess Openings*, considered 8 ... ♘d7! to be more precise, transposing to B after 9 ♕d3 ♗e7, and supposedly avoiding the main line in A. However, he did not say explicitly how Black should meet 9 f4. If 9 ... ef 10 ♗×f4 ♕b6+ 11 ♔h1, for example, 11 ... ♕×b2 12 ♕d2 still seems risky, while 11 ... ♘e5 practically fails outright against 12 ♗×e5 de 13 ♗c4 f6? 14 ♖×f6! gf 15 ♕h5+ ♔d8 16 ♕f7! – AHM.

67
W

A 9 f4
B 9 ♕d3!

a) **9 ♔h1** (loss of tempo) 9 ... 00 10 f4 ♘d7 11 f5 ♗b7 12 ♕d3 ♘b6 13 a4 (13 ♗e3 d5!) 13 ... a5 14 ♗e3= – S.

b) **9 ♗c4** 00 10 ♕e2 ♕c7 11 h3 ♗b7 12 ♗g5 h6 13 ♗×f6 ♗×f6 14 ♖ad1 ♖ab8 15 ♖d3 ♗a8 16 b3 a5 17 ♕g4 ♖bd8∓ (two bishops) Morel–Boleslavsky, Helsinki 1952.

**A**

**9 f4**              **♘d7!**

Others:

a) **9 ... 00** 10 ♔h1 ♘d7 11 ♗c4 ♕c7 12 ♕h5!?± Winston–Schneider, World Junior Ch, Manila 1974.

b) **9 ... ef!?** 10 ♗×f4 ♕b6+ 11 ♔h1 and now:

b1) **11 ... ♕×b2?** 12 ♕d3 ♕b4 (12 ... ♕a3!± – R, 1952) 13 ♖ab1 ♕c5 14 ♘a4 ♕a5 15 ♗×d6 ♕×a4 16♗×e 7 ♔×e7 17 e5 ♘e8 18 ♕c3 ♘c7 19 ♕c5+ ♔e8 20 ♕d6 ♘d5 21 ♗b5! c6 22 ♕×d5 1–0 Berquist–Poulsen, Stockholm v. Copenhagen radio match 1952.

b2) **11 ... 00** 12 ♕d3 (12 ♗×d6 ♗×d6 13 ♕×d6 ♕×b2) 12 ... ♗e6 13 ♕g3± e.g. 13 ... ♕×b2? 14 ♖ab1! ♕×c2 (14 ... ♕a3? 15 ♘d5!) 15 ♖fc1 ♘×e4 16 ♖×c2 – R.

10 f5

If 10 ♕d3 ef 11 ♗×f4 ♘e5 12 ♕g3 then either 12 ... 00 (B2) or 12 ... ♘d7 – G.

10 ...                    00
11 ♕d3                  ♗b7

Or 11 ... ♘b6!? 12 ♕g3 when:

a) **12 ... d5?** 13 ♗h6 (13 ♕×e5!±) 13 ... ♗f6 14 ♗×g7? ♗h4 15 ♗f6+ ♗×g3 16 ♗×d8 ♗×h2+ 17 ♔×h2 ♖×d8= – S.

b) **12 ... ♗h4** 13 ♕g4 ♔h8 14 ♖f3 with a strong attack, according to Barden. Donner–Trott, Beverwijk 1953, however continued 14 ... g6 15 ♖h3 ♗f6 16

♗d2 d5 17 ♖f1 ♖b8 18 ♖1f3 ♖b7 ½–½. Could White have done better?

12 ♕g3      d5!
13 ♗h6

S also gives:

a) **13 ♔h1** d4! 14 ♘d1 c5∓.
b) **13 ♗d3** ♗f6 intending ... c5!∓.

13 ...      ♗f6
14 ♖ad1      ♔h8
15 ♗c1      d4
16 ♘b1      c5∓

Fuller–Taimanov, Hastings 1955–6; Black has a solid position and Q-side targets. White's control of c4 can easily be contested.

**B**

**9 ♕d3!** *(68)*

This was an idea of the Czech master Louma – to engage the queen and strengthen control of the centre, hoping to inhibit ... d5.

68
B

B1 9 ... 00
B2 9 ... ♘d7!

9 ... ♗e6? 10 f4 ef 11 ♗×f4 00 12 ♖ad1± – S.

**B1**

9 ...      00

B11 10 ♖d1
B12 10 ♕g3
B13 10 f4!

10 ♗g5 ♖b8 11 b3 ♗e6 12 ♖ad1 ♕a5:

a) **13 ♘a4?** d5∓ Louma–Gragger, Vienna 1949.
b) **13 ♕g3** ♖fd8= – P.

**B11**

10 ♖d1      ♘d7

Probably better 10 ... ♕c7 (or 10 ... ♕d7) 11 f4 (11 ♗g5 ♖d8= – Pachman) 11 ... ♖d8 12 ♕g3 ♗b7 13 b3 ♘e8 14 ♗b2 ♗f6 15 ♘a4 ef 16 ♕×f4= Louma–Kottnauer, Bratislava 1948.

11 ♗e3

Others:

a) **11 f4?!** ♕b6+ 12 ♔h1 ef 13 ♗×f4 ♘e5 14 ♕g3 f6∓ Rovner–Kopayev, Vilnius ½-final 17th USSR Ch 1948.
b) **11 ♕g3** ♔h8 12 f4 ♕c7 13 b3 a5 14 ♘a4 f5= Gretchkin–Ilivitsky, Vilnius ½-final 17th USSR Ch 1948.

11 ...      ♘b6
12 a4      ♗e6
13 b3      a5

14 f4 f6 15 f5 ♗f7 16 ♗f3 ♕c7 17 ♕e2 ♖fd8 18 ♕f2± Louma–Foltys, Bratislava 1948.

**B12**

10 ♕g3      ♗e6?!

Possibly better:

a) **10 ... ♘d7!** see B2.
b) **10 ... ♖b8** 11 b3 ♘d7 12

♖d1 ♘c5 13 f4 ♕b6 14 ♔h1
♔h8= Pytlakowski–Taimanov,
Sczawno Zdroj 1950.

c) **10 ... ♔h8** 11 f4 ♕b6+
12 ♔h1 ef= Unzicker–Rabar,
Lucerne 1949.

d) **10 ... ♘e8** and if 11 f4 ♗f6
12 f5 ♘c7 (preparing ... d5) – B.

     11 f4           ef

     12 ♗×f4

Black has difficulties with his
d-pawn:

a) **12 ... ♘e8** 13 ♖ad1± Hort–
Shamkovich, Moscow 1962.

b) **12 ... ♘d7** 13 ♖ad1! – B.

c) **12 ... ♕b6+** 13 ♔h1 ♕×b2
14 ♖ab1 ♕a3 (14 ... ♕×c2 15
♖fc1) 15 ♘d5±± – B.

**B13**

     **10 f4!**          ♘d7

10 ... ef 11 ♗×f4 ♕b6+ fails
as in the previous note.

     11 ♗g4

As G points out, White has the
opportunity here (but not in B2)
to prevent Black's knight reaching
the strong post e5. R's suggestion
of 11 f5 (and 12 ♕g3) also
satisfies this condition.

     11 ...           ♕b6+?!

11 ... ♘c5! is critical:

a) **12 ♕f3** ♕b6 13 ♔h1 ♗×g4
14 ♕×g4 ♘×e4! 15 ♘×e4 f5
16 ♕e2 fe 17 ♕×e4 ♗f6 – Rabar
in R, 1950

b) **12 ♕g3** ♗×g4 13 ♕×g4
♘×e4 14 ♘×e4 f5 15 ♕e2 fe
16 ♕×e4 (16 ♕c4+ d5 17
♕×c6 ♖c8∓) 16 ... d5! 17
♕×e5 ♕b6+ 18 ♔h1 (18 ♗e3

♗c5 19 ♗×c5 ♕×c5+ 20
♔h1 ♖ae8) 18 ... ♖ae8 and
Black has a strong position in
return for the pawn sacrificed – B.

     12 ♗e3!          ♘c5

     13 ♗×c8         ♘×d3

     14 ♗×c5         ♖f×c8

     15 cd           dc

16 f5 b5 17 a4!± Janošević–
Rabar, Yugoslav Ch 1949.

**B2**

     **9 ...**          **♘d7!** (69)

The one sure equalizing line.

**69
W**

     10 ♕g3

Also:

a) **10 f4** ef 11 ♗×f4 ♘e5 (11 ...
♕b6+? 12 ♔h1 ♕×b2? 13
♕c4!±) and Black's knight has
reached the centre in time, e.g.
12 ♕g3 ♘g6 – R, 1952

b) According to R, relatively best
for White is **10 ♗e3** (deterring
... ♘c5) 10 ... 00 11 ♖ad1 a5
12 ♕c4 ♗b7 with about equal
chances.

c) **10 ♖d1!?** ♘c5 (10 ... 00 see
B11) 11 ♕g3 00 gives Black a
good fighting game, e.g. 12 f4

♕b6 13 ♔h1 f5!? 14 fe de! – AHM.

10 ...        00
11 f4

Or 11 ♗h6?! ♘f6 12 ♖ad1 ♘c5 13 ♗c4 ♘e6 14 ♗c1 ♘d4∓ Bogoljubow – Gligorić, Staunton Memorial 1951.

11 ...        ef
12 ♗×f4

a) 12 ... ♘c5 13 ♗c4 ♘e6 14 ♗e3 ♘f6 15 ♖ad1 ♗e5 16 ♕f2 ♕a5 17 ♗×e6 ♗×e6 18 ♗d4= Walther–Euwe, Zürich 1954.

b) 12 ... ♘e5! 13 ♗×e5 (13 ♖ad1 ♕c7= – B) 13 ... de 14 ♕×e5 ♗d6 15 ♕h5 ♕b6+ 16 ♔h1 ♕×b2∓ – G.

## Conclusion

The Boleslavsky is a good variation but there are few opportunities for playing it nowadays. None of the lines in this chapter are dangerous, except for Louma's plan (B) which is to be countered by the ... ♘d7 manoeuvre as in B2.

# 8 Boleslavsky, 7 ♘f3

After 1 e4 c5 2 ♘f3 ♘c6 3 d4 cd 4 ♘×d4 ♘f6 5 ♘c3 d6 6 ♗e2 e5 the retreat 7 ♘f3 (70) has perhaps been under-rated. It is true that White commits himself to a rather rigid formation, renouncing the chance of a brisk f4. On the other hand, Black's choices are also restricted; in the first place, he has to meet the positional threat of ♗g5, ♗×f6 and ♘d5 which would seize control of d5. Then he will find that the ♘f3 exerts pressure on e5, making it difficult to achieve the freeing ... d5 advance. In practice Black has usually found sufficient resources, but it is to this line rather than the more popular 7 ♘b3 that

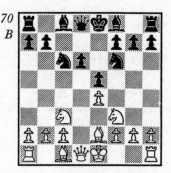

70
B

White should look first for improvements.

    7 ...        h6

7 ... ♗e7 8 ♗g5! e.g.:

a) **8 ... ♗g4** (playing for opposite colour bishops) 9 ♗×f6 ♗×f6 10 ♘d5 ♗×f3 (or 10 ... 00 11 00 ♖c8 12 c3) 11 ♗×f3 ♘e7 12 ♘×f6+ gf 13 00± – K.

b) **8 ... 00** when:

b1) **9 ♗×f6!?** and 10 ♘d5 – S.

b2) **9 00** ♗e6 10 ♕d2 h6 11 ♗×f6 ♗×f6 12 ♖fd1 ♕a5 13 ♘d5± – B.

b3) **9 ♕d2** ♗e6 10 ♖d1 ♕a5 11 00:

b31) **11 ... a6?** 12 ♗×f6 ♗×f6 (12 ... gf 13 ♕h6) 13 ♘d5 ♗×d5 (13 ... ♕×d2 14 ♘×f6+ gf 15 ♖×d2 ♖fd8 16 ♖fd1) 14 ♕×a5 ♘×a5 15 ♖×d5 ♘c6 16 ♖×d6± L. Steiner–Pirc, Saltsjöbaden interzonal 1948.

b32) **11 ... ♖fd8** 12 ♗×f6 ♗×f6 13 ♘d5 (± Kuzminikh in *Shakhmaty v SSSR*, 1951) 13 ... ♕×d2 14 ♖×d2 ♗×d5 15 ♖×d5 ♘b4= e.g. 16 ♖b5 (16 ♖d2 d5!) 16 ... ♘×c2 17 ♖×b7 ♖db8= – S.

7 ... ♗e7 would be good if
White forgot to play ♗g5, e.g.
Yanofsky – Pirc, Saltsjöbaden
interzonal 1948, which continued
8 00 00 9 b3?! ♗g4 10 ♗b2
♖c8 11 h3 ♗×f3 12 ♗×f3 ♘d4
13 ♕d3 ♕a5 14 ♗d1 ♘e6 15 a3
a6 16 ♖c1 b5 17 b4 ♕b6∓.
Unfortunately the evidence above
tends to show that Black must
'lose' a tempo in playing 7 ... h6
lest his position be deadened by
loss of control of d5.

After 7 ... h6:

A 8 ♗c4
B 8 00

a) **8 ♘d2** d5 9 ♘×d5 ♘×d5
10 ed ♕×d5 11 00 ♗e6 12 c3
♗e7 13 ♗c4 ♕d7 14 ♕b3 ♗×c4
15 ♘×c4 ♖d8 16 ♗e3 00 17
♖ad1 ♕e6= Puc–Ivkov, Yugoslav Ch 1958.

b) **8 h3** ♗e7 (8 ... ♗e6 and 9 ...
d5 is better – K.) 9 ♘h2!? ♗e6 (9
... ♘d4!? – Milić, *Informator* 6)
10 ♘g4 00 11 ♗e3 ♕d7 12
♘×f6+ ♗×f6 (Letzelter–
Benko, Lugano Olympiad 1968)
13 ♗g4! intending 14 ♘d5± –
Milić.

c) **8 b3** ♗e6 9 00 see B1.

d) **8 ♗e3** ♗e7 (or 8 ... ♗e6 9 00
♗e7) 9 00 see B21.

**A**

8 ♗c4 *(71)*
8 ...　　　　♗e7
9 h3

Avoiding 9 00 ♗g4! 10 ♗e3
♖c8 11 ♗b3 00∓ – S.
9 ...　　　　00

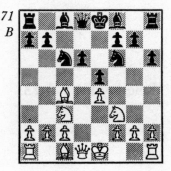

71
B

10 00　　　　♗e6
11 ♗b3

Others:

a) **11 ♕e2** ♖c8 12 ♗b3 ♘a5 13
♖d1 ♕c7 14 g4? ♘×b3 15 ab a6
16 ♕h1 b5 17 b4 ♕c4∓ Stoltz–
Boleslavsky, Groningen 1946.

b) **11 ♗×e6** fe 12 ♘h4? ♘×e4
13 ♘g6 ♘×c3∓.

11 ...　　　　♘a5
12 ♗d5!

Or 12 ♖e1:

a) **12 ... ♘×b3** 13 ab ♕c7 14
♗e3 a6 15 ♕d3 b5∓ L. Steiner–
Bronstein, Saltsjöbaden interzonal 1948.

b) **12 ... ♖c8** 13 ♗e3 ♘c4 14
♗×c4 ♖×c4∓ – S.

12 ...　　　　♗×d5
13 ♘×d5!　　♖c8

Not 13 ... ♘×e4? 14 ♘×e7+
♕×e7 15 ♕e1±±.

14 ♘×f6+　　♗×f6
15 c3　　　　♕d7
16 ♘h2　　　♗d8=

Voronov – Kuzminikh, ½-final
Leningrad Ch 1948.

**B**

**8 00**

B1 8 ... ♗e6
B2 8 ... ♗e7
**B1**

**8 ...          ♗e6**
Playing for a quick ... d5.
9 ♖e1!
Puts indirect pressure on e5. Other critical lines:
a) 9 ♗e3 d5!? (9 ... ♗e7 B21) when:
a1) 10 ♗b5? d4 11 ♘×e5 de 12 ♘×c6 bc 13 ♗×c6+ ♗d7 14 ♗×a8 ef+ 15 ♔h1 ♕×a8∓ – P.
a2) 10 ed! ♘×d5 (= S) 11 ♘×d5 ♕×d5 12 ♕×d5 ♗×d5 13 ♖ed1 with the better endgame for White – G.
b) 9 b3!? d5!? (9 ... ♗e7 10 ♕d2 00 B23) 10 ♗b5 (± S) 10 ... d4 11 ♘×e5 dc 12 ♘×c6 bc 13 ♗×c6+ ♗d7 14 ♗×a8 ♕×a8 with an obscure position in which Black's two bishops may have some value. Possibly 15 a4!? and 16 ♗a3 is best now – AHM.

9 ...          ♗e7
Not 9 ... d5? 10 ed ♘×d5 11 ♘×d5 ♕×d5 12 ♕cd5 ♗×d5 13 ♘×e5! ♘×e5 14 ♗b5+±± – B.

10 ♗f1          ♗g4
10 ... d5? puts the e-pawn en prise, while 10 ... 00 transposes to Yudovich–Boleslavsky in B22.
11 ♗e3
Or 11 h3 ♗×f3 12 ♕×f3 ♘d4= – S.
11 ...          00
12 h3          ♗×f3

13 ♕×f3±
Play might go on 13 ... d5!? 14 ed ♘b4 15 ♖ed1 ♘×c2 16 ♖ac1 ♘×e3 17 fe:
a) 17 ... ♗c5? 18 ♔h1 ♖c8 19 ♗d3 with attacking chances;
b) 17 ... ♗d6 18 ♗d3 ♕b6 19 ♖c2 ♖c8 20 ♔h1 ♖c7 21 ♖f2, with the idea of ♕e2, ♖1f1 and possible sacrifices on f6. Thanks to his K-side chances and central passed pawn, only White has chances of winning in this line – K.

**B2**
8 ...          ♗e7 (72)
Preferring to free the position slowly, keeping open all the options of the queen's bishop and getting the king into safety.

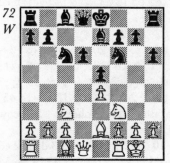

72
W

B21 9 ♗e3
B22 9 ♖e1
B23 9 b3
a) 9 ♕d3 00 10 ♘e1 (or 10 ♖d1 ♗e6= – S) 10 ... ♗e6 11 ♕g3 ♔h8 12 f4 ♘d4 13 ♗d1 ♗c4 14 ♘d3 d5 15 fe ♘×e4 Kopayev–Kuzminikh, USSR Trade Union Team Ch 1947.

b) **9 ♘e1!?** ♗e6 10 f4 was once proposed by Pachman.

c) **9 h3** 00 see below.

**B21**

      **9 ♗e3**

This simple development fails to stop ... d5 in the long run.

      **9 ...**      **00**

Or 9 ... ♗e6 10 ♕d2 (10 ♘e1 below) 10 ... d5? (10 ... 00 below) 11 ed ♘×d5 12 ♗b5!± Paoli – Kottnauer, Trenčianske Teplice 1949.

      **10 ♕d2**

Others:

a) **10 ♖e1** ♗e6 11 ♗b5 a6 12 ♗a4 (Rellstab–Berquist, Dubrovnik Olympiad 1950) 12 ... ♘a5!∓ – G.

b) **10 h3** ♗e6 11 ♕d2 a6 12 ♖ad1 b5 13 a3 ♖c8 14 ♕c1 ♖e8 15 ♖fe1 ♗f8 16 ♗f1 ♕a5 17 ♖d2 ♘b8 18 ♘d5 ♘×e4 19 ♗b6 ♘×d2 20 ♗×a5 ♘×f3+ 21 gf ♗×d5 22 f4 (22 ♗g2!? ♘c6 23 ♗c3) 22 ... ♖e6 23 ♗c3 ♖g6+ 24 ♔h2 ♘d7 (0–1, 45) Tarasov–Makarichev, Moscow 1972.

c) **10 ♘e1** ♗e6 11 ♘d3 d5! 12 ed ♘×d5 13 ♘×d5 ♗×d5 14 ♗c5? (better 14 ♕d2 – Barden) 14 ... ♗×c5 15 ♘×c5 ♘d4!∓ e.g. 16 ♘b3 ♕g5 17 f3 ♕e3+ 18 ♖f2 ♗×b3 19 ab ♖fd8 20 ♗d3 ♘×c2! 21 ♗h7+ ♔×h7 22 ♕×c2+ ♔g8 23 ♔f1 ♖ac8 24 ♖e1 ♖×c2 0–1 Radulescu–Foltys, Budapest 1948.

      **10 ...**      **♗e6**

      **11 ♖ad1** (*73*)

A critical position, in which lots of moves have been proposed.

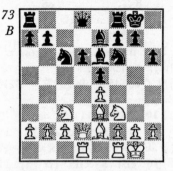

73
B

a) **11 ...** **♘a5** 12 ♘d5! ♗×d5 13 ed ♖c8 (13 ... b6 14 b4 ♘b7 15 c4± – S) 14 ♗×a7 b6 15 ♕b4 ♘d7 16 ♗b5 ♘c5 17 ♗d3 ♘d7 18 ♗f5 ♘c4 19 b3 ♕c7 20 ♕×c4 ♕×a7 21 ♕b5± Bronstein–Boleslavsky, 15th USSR Ch 1947.

b) **11 ...** **a6!?** 12 h3! b5 13 a3 ♕b8 14 ♘h2 ♕b7 15 ♘g+! (± S) 15 ... ♗×g4 16 hg b4? 17 ab ♘×b4 18 f3 ♖fc8 19 b3!± (1–0, 40) Unzicker–Bogoljubow, W. German club match 1951.

c) **11 ...** **♖e8** 12 h3 ♖c8= Levenfish–Boleslavsky, Kuibyshev 1943.

d) **11 ...** **♕d7!** (or first 11 ... ♖c8!? – Kuzminikh) when G comments: 'Black has a fluid position. For example, 12 h3 ♖fd8 13 ♘h2? d5 or 12 ♕e1 ♖ac8 etc. The centre is successfully fixed, and Black controls the critical squares.' After 11 ... ♕d7 12 ♕e1 Black can also consider

12 ... ♖fd8 13 ♗c1 (13 ♘d2
♘d4!=) 13 ... ♗f8 14 b3
♕c8= as given by Barden and S.

**B22**

   **9 ♖e1**      **00**
   **10 h3**

Others:

a) **10 b3** a6 11 a4 ♗e6 12 ♗b2
♖c8 13 h3 ♕a5 14 ♗f1 ♖fd8=
Castaldi–Unzicker, Munich 1954.
b) **10 ♗f1!** when:
b1) **10 ... ♗e6** and now:
b11) **11 b3?** ♖c8 12 ♗b2 ♗g4
13 ♗e2 ♗×f3 14 ♗×f3 ♘d4 15
♕d3 ♕a5∓ Taimanov–Bron-
stein, 16th USSR Ch 1948.
b12) **11 h3** ♖c8 (Yudovich–
Boleslavsky, Moscow Ch 1942)
12 ♘d5± e.g. 12 ... ♗×d5 13 ed
♘b4 14 c4 – R, 1952.
b2) **10 ... a6!** 11 a4! is critical.
Should Black play 11 ... b6, 11 ...
♗e6 or 11 ... ♗g4!? If White
does not fear ... ♗g4, why
should he play h3!

   **10 ...**      **a6**
   **11 ♗f1**

Broadbent–Unzicker, Staunton
Memorial 1951, went 11 a4 ♗e6
12 b3 ♖c8 13 ♗a3 ♕a5 14 ♕d2
♘d4! 15 ♗b2 ♘×e2+ 16
♖×e2∓.

   **11 ...**      **b5**
   **12 a3**

Or 12 a4 b4 13 ♘d5
(Taimanov – Ilivitsky, USSR
Team Ch 1949) 13 ... ♗b7 with
a good game for Black – G.

   **12 ...**      **♗b7**
   **13 b3**      **♖c8**

14 ♗b2      ♖c7∓

It is hard to find a plan for
White. Unzicker – Taimanov,
Stockholm 1952, continued 15
♘b1 (15 ♘d5 ♘×d5 16 ed
♘b8∓ – Sokolsky) 15 ... ♕a8!
16 ♘bd2 ♘d8 17 ♗d3 ♘e6 18
♖c1 ♖fc8 19 ♘h2 ♘d7 20
♘hf1 ♘dc5 21 ♘g3 g6 22 ♘e2
♗g5 23 ♘c3 ♘d4 24 ♘cb1 d5!
25 ed ♘×d3 26 cd ♖×c1 27
♗×c1 ♗×d5 28 f3 ♖c2! 29
a4 (29 ♖×e5 ♗×f3!) 29 ... b4
30 ♔h1 ♕c6! 0–1 (zugzwang).

**B23**

   **9 b3**      **00**

Perhaps 9 ... ♗g4 is best – K.
   **10 ♗b2 (74)**

Once more, White tries for
indirect pressure on e5.

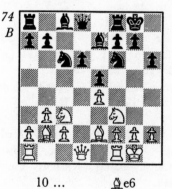

   **10 ...**      **♗e6**

Others:

a) **10 ... ♗g4** 11 ♖e1 ♖c8 12 h3
♗×f3 13 ♗×f3 ♘d4 14 ♕d3 b5
15 ♗d1! (Smyslov–Ciocaltea,
Moscow 1956) may favour White,
although R suggested 15 ... a6
16 a4 ♕b6 17 ♘e2 ♘e6 18 ab ab
etc.

b) **10 ... a6!?** when:

b1) **11 ♕d2** b5 12 a3 ♗b7∓ – B.

b2) **11 a4!** e.g. 11 ... b6 12 ♖e1 ♗b7 13 ♕d2 ♖c8 14 ♖ad1 ♕c7 15 ♗c4 ♕b8 16 ♘h4 ♖fd8 17 ♘f5 ♗f8 18 ♖e3± Benson–Kiviaho, corres 1973–5.

11 ♕d2
B231 11 ... a6
B232 11 ... ♖c8

**B231**

    **11 ...**     **a6**
    12 h3

Or:

a) **12 a4** ♖c8 13 ♖ad1 ♖e8 14 h3 Alexander–Puc, Belgrade 1952.

b) **12 ♖fe1** ♖e8 13 ♖ad1 ♗f8 14 ♗f1? (14 h3 – R) 14 ... ♗g4 15 ♗e2 ♖c8∓ Podgorny–Stoltz, Karlovy Vary 1948.

    12 ...     ♕a5
    13 ♖fd1

Or 13 ♖ad1 ♖ac8 14 a3 ♖fd8 15 ♖fe1 ♗f8 16 ♗f1 (± – P) 16 ... b5= – S.

    13 ...     ♖ac8
    14 a3     ♖fd8
    15 ♖ac1     ♗f8

16 ♕e3 b5 17 ♘d5 ♗×d5 18 ed ♘e7 19 c4 bc 20 bc ♘d7= Yanofsky–Sajtar, Karlovy Vary 1948.

**B232**

    **11 ...**     **♖c8**
    12 ♖fd1

Others:

a) **12 ♖ad1** ♕a5 13 h3 ♖fd8 14 ♕e3 a6 15 a4 (15 a3 b5 16 ♘d5 is unclear – S.) 15 ... ♖d7= Koginov – Kopilov, Leningrad

1952; note that with the queen's rook still at a1, 15 a3 would be good as ... b5 is then met by ab.

b) **12 h3!** is the most precise choice.

    12 ...     a6

If 12 ... ♕a5 13 h3 ♖fd8 14 ♕e3! becomes a promising idea. It all hinges on whether Black can play 14 ... d5 safely, e.g. 15 ed ♘×d5 16 ♘×d5 ♖×d5 17 ♖×d5 ♕×d5 18 ♗c4 ♕d7= – K.

    13 a4     ♘b4

But surely Black should play 13 ... ♗g4! (or even 12 ... ♗g4), to take advantage of the absence of White's queen's bishop from the e3–a7 diagonal. Black gets a useful knight at d4, and White's c-pawn becomes weak – K.

    14 ♖ac1     ♕b6
    15 ♗a3     a5
    16 ♗b5     ♖×c3!

17 ♕×c3 ♗×f2+! 18 ♔×f2 (18 ♔h1 ♘×e4 19 ♕e1 f5) 18 ... ♘×e4+ 19 ♔g1 ♘×c3 20 ♖de1 ♖c8 (20 ... f5 21 ♘d4!) 21 ♗×b4 ab 22 ♗d3 g6 23 ♖a1 ♗f6! 24 ♖fc1 (24 a5 e4 25 a6 ba 26 ♗×a6 ♖a8!) 24 ... ♗d5!∓ Limbos – Spanjaard, Beverwijk 1951; a pleasing but somewhat fortuitous combination!

Conclusion

In these lines where White puts his efforts into preventing ... d5, Black's best plan is to fight for control of d4 with ... ♗g4 if

White fianchettos his queen's bishop (as in B23), or to advance on the Q-side with ... a6, ... b5 etc. (as in Unzicker–Taimanov, p. 83) as long as White is not well placed to block this with a4. It is possible that 7 ♘f3 has been under-estimated in the past, and is White's best chance against the Boleslavsky.

## 9 Boleslavsky, 7 ♘b3

After 1 e4 c5 2 ♘f3 ♘c6 3 d4 cd 4 ♘×d4 ♘f6 5 ♘c3 d6 6 ♗e2 e5 White most often plays 7 ♘b3 (75). In this way, White keeps the options of ♗f3 or f4 and retains control of the g4 square. On the darker side, the knight has nothing particular to do at b3 and can become the target for a tempo-gaining advance of Black's a-pawn.

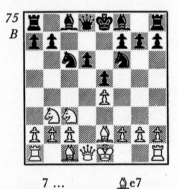

75
B

7 ...                ♗e7

Others are premature:

a) 7 ... ♗e6 8 ♗g5 ♗e7 9 00:

a1) 9 ... ♘×e4? 10 ♘×e4 ♗×g5 11 ♘×d6+ ♔e7 12 ♘×b7±± – S.

a2) 9 ... 00 10 ♗×f6 ♗×f6 11 ♘d5 ♗×d5 12 ♕×d5 ♕c7 13 c3 ♖fd8 14 ♗c4! ♖ac8 15 ♘d2 ♘a5 16 ♗b3± – S.

b) 7 ... a5!? when:

b1) 8 ♗b5!? ♗e7 9 00 00 10 ♕e2 d5 11 ed ♘×d5 12 ♘×d5 ♕×d5 13 ♗e3 ♗f5 14 ♖fd1 ♕e6 15 ♘c5 ♗×c5 16 ♗×c5± Bastrikov–Kuz, USSR Trade Union Team Ch 1949.

b2) 8 00 a4 9 ♘d2 d5 10 ed ♘×d5 11 ♘×d5 ♕×d5 12 ♗f3± – Kuzminikh.

b3) 8 a4 ♗e6 (8 ... ♗e7 9 ♗g5 00 10 ♗×f6 ♗×f6 11 ♘d5 ♗g5 12 c3± – S) 9 ♗g5 ♗e7 10 ♗×f6 ♗×f6 11 ♘d5 00 (11 ... ♘b4? 12 ♗b5+!± – S) 12 ♗g4 ♗g5 13 c3:

b31) 13 ... ♘e7 14 ♘×e7+ ♕×e7 15 00± (½–½, 38) O'Kelly–Tartakower, Groningen 1946.

b32) 13 ... g6! 14 00 f5 15 ♗h3 ♘e7 16 g3 ♘×d5 (0–1, 41) Nordstrom v. Skurovich–Hazin, Sweden v. USSR corres 1970–2.

c) 7 ... h6 would be redundant, as ♗g5 is not dangerous after the text move.

After 7 ... ♗e7:

A 8 ♗g5

B 8 h4!?
C 8 ♗e3
D 8 00
a) **8 g4?!** 00! 9 g5 ♘e8 10 ♗e3
♗e6 11 ♕d2 f5!∓ – Filip.
b) **8 f3** when:
b1) **8 ... a5** 9 ♗e3 a4 10 ♘d2 a3
11 b3 ♕a5 12 ♘b5 d5 13 00 00
14 c3 ♗e6∓ Nikolić–Parma,
Yugoslav Ch 1965.
b2) **8 ... d5!?** 9 ♘×d5 ♘×d5
10 ed ♘b4 11 ♗b5+ (11 c4
♗f5) 11 ... ♔f8∓ – Pachman.

**A**

**8 ♗g5**(76)
Compared with 7 ♘f3 lines,
the bishop is not protected now.

76
B

8 ...          00!?
This allows White to execute
his 'threat', judging that the
strong bishop at g5 will be
compensation for the loss of d5.
However Black has also a per-
fectly safe line in 8 ... ♘×e4,
e.g.:
a) **9 ♗×e7** ♘×c3 10 ♗×d8
♘×d1 11 ♖×d1 ♔×d8 12
♖×d6+:

a1) **12 ... ♔e7**= Böök–Bronstein,
Saltsjöbaden interzonal 1948.
a2) **12 ... ♔c7!**∓ Ivkov–Gligorić,
Yugoslav Ch 1951.
b) **9 ♘×e4** ♗×g5 10 ♘×d6+
(or 10 ♘×g5 ♕×g5 11 ♕×d6
♕e7=) 10 ... ♔e7 11 ♘e4
♗h6 12 00 f5 13 ♘g3 ♕×d1=
Bivshev–Vatnikov, Vilnius ½-final
17th USSR Ch 1949
9 ♗×f6
Others:
a) **9 ♕d2** a5 10 a3 a4 11 ♘c1 ♗e6
12 00 ♘d4 13 ♖d1 ♖c8∓
Kasparian–Geller, USSR 1952.
b) **9 00** ♘e8 (9 ... ♘×e4!? 10
♘×e4 ♗×g5 11 ♕×d6=) 10
♗×e7 ♘×e7:
b1) **11 f4** ♕b6+ 12 ♔h1 ♘f6
13 a4 a5 14 ♘d2 ♕×b2 15 ♘b5
♕b4∓ Kirillov–Kuzminikh, ½-
final 16th USSR Ch 1947.
b2) **11 ♗f3** ♗e6 12 ♕d2 a6 13
♖ad1 ♖c8 14 ♖fe1 ♕c7=
Vinogradov – Kuzminikh, Leningrad Ch 1947.
9 ...          ♗×f6
10 ♘d5
Or 10 00 ♗e6 11 ♘d5 ♗g5
12 ♕d3 (12 00 a5 or 12 ♗b5!?)
12 ... ♘e7 13 c4? ♖c8 14 ♘d2
♘×d5 15 cd ♗d7 16 ♘c4 ♕c7
17 a4 b5 18 ab ♗×b5∓
Taimanov – Boleslavsky, 17th
USSR Ch 1949.
10 ...          ♗g5!
Or 10 ... ♗e6!? Rudzitis–
Vitolins, corres 1973.
11 ♗c4          ♗e6
12 h4

Or 12 00 a5.

12 ...              ♗h6
13 g4?            ♗f4!

Suetin comments, in *Modern Chess Opening Theory*, that 'In spite of White's temporary occupation of d5, Black has the better chances, because his pieces are well co-ordinated'. Reicher–Boleslavsky, Bucharest 1953, went on: 14 ♕e2 ♖c8 15 c3 ♘e7 16 ♖d1 ♘g6 17 h5 (17 g5 h5!) 17 ... ♘h4 18 ♗d3 ♕g5 19 f3 ♗g3+ 20 ♔f1 f5! 21 ♖g1 ♘×f3! 22 ♖×g3! fe 23 ♔g2 ed 24 ♖×d3 ♗×d5 25 ♖×d5 ♕h4! 26 ♖×f3 ♕×g4+ 0–1.

**B**

**8 h4!?** *(77)*

Still pursuing the idea of occupying d5. Tricky play results.

77
B

8 ...              00!

As recommended by G: the white pieces (♗e2, ♘b3 etc.) are hardly well placed to attack Black's king.

Others justify White's move:
a) **8 ... a5** 9 ♗g5 a4 10 ♘c1 a3

11 b3 ♗e6 12 ♘b5!?± – AHM.
b) **8 ... h6** 9 g4 ♗e6 10 g5 hg 11 ♗×g5:
b1) **11 ... ♕d7** 12 ♕d2 000 13 000± Djaja–Marković, Belgrade 1949.
b2) **11 ... a5** ♗b5 a4 13 ♗×a4 ♘×e4 14 ♗×c6+ bc 15 ♘×e4 ♗×g5 16 ♘×g5 ♕×g5 17 ♕×d6±± Djaja–Marić, Novi Sad 1949.

9 g4

G's comment that 9 ♗g5 is line A with a tempo more for Black is not strictly correct, since after 9 ... ♗e6 10 ♗×f6 ♗×f6 11 g3! his bishop is denied the use of the thematic g5 square. Nevertheless, White's backward development can be exploited by 11 ... a5! 12 ♘d5 (12 a4 ♘b4 and ... d5) 12 ... a4 13 ♘×f6+ (13 ♘c1 ♘d4) 13 ... ♕×f6 14 ♘c1 ♖fd8 15 c4 (else ... d5) 15 ... ♘d4 with good piece play – AHM.

9 ...              ♘e8!

9 ... d5?! appears unsound, because of 10 ed ♘b4 11 ♗f3 e4!? 12 ♘×e4:
a) **12 ... ♘×e4** 13 ♗×e4 ♗×h4 14 g5±
b) **12 ... ♖e8** 13 ♘×f6+ ♗×f6+ 14 ♔f1 ♗×h4 15 c3± – AHM

10 g5              ♗e6

continuing with ... f5 and a good position – AHM.

**C**

**8 ♗e3**          00 *(78)*

78
W

9 f3!?
a) **9 00** see D4.
b) **9 g4?!** a5 10 g5 (10 a4 ♘b4)
10 ... ♘e8:
b1) **11 ♘d5** ♗×g5 12 ♗b6 ♕d7
13 ♖g1 f6 14 ♗g4 ♕f7 15
♗×c8 ♖×c8 16 ♘×a5 ♘e7!∓
Vinogradov – Boleslavsky, Sverdlovsk Ch 1943.
b2) **11 h4** a4 12 ♘d2 a3 13 b3
♘b4 14 ♗c4 ♗e6∓ – B.
c) **9 ♗f3!?** a6? (9 ... a5! –
Shamkovich) 10 g4!?:
c1) **10 ...** ♗e6 11 ♘d5! ♗×d5
12 ed ♘a5 13 g5 ♘d7 14 ♘×a5
♕×a5 15 ♕d2! ♕a4 16 ♖g1
♖ac8 17 b3 ♕a3 18 ♗g4 ♖fd8
19 h4 ♖c7 20 h5 g6 21 hg hg
22 ♗×d7 ♖d×d7 23 ♔e2 ♖c8
24 f4! (1–0, 39) Baikov–
Makarichev, Daugavpils 1974.
c2) **10 ... a5!?** 11 g5 ♘e8 12
♘d5 a4 is unclear – Shamkovich,
*Chess Player* 6
d) **9 ♕d2** ♗e6 (9 ... ♗g4 10
♗×g4 or 9 ... a5 10 ♖d1) 10
♖d1 ♘a5 (only playable when
White hasn't castled) 11 ♘×a5
♕×a5= e.g. 12 f3 ♖fd8 13

♘d5 ♕×d2+ 14 ♖×d2 ♘×d5
15 ed ♗d7 16 00 ♖dc8 17 c4
♗d8∓ – K.
9 ...                    d5
Others:
a) **9 ...** ♗e6 10 ♘d5 ♗×d5 11
ed ♘b4 12 c4 b5? (12 ... a5!?)
13 a3 bc 14 ♗×c4 ♖c8 15
♖c1± – S.
b) **9 ... a5** 10 ♘a4 ♗e6 11 c4
♘d7 12 ♕d2 b6 13 00 ♘c5 14
♘c3 a4 15 ♘c1 ♕d7 16 ♖b1 f5
17 b4 ab 18 ab fe 19 fe ♖×f1+
20 ♗×f1 ♘b4 21 ♘a4 ♘×a4
22 ba ♘c6 23 ♖×b6 ♖×a4 24
c5 ♗d8 25 ♖b2 dc 26 ♗b5 ♖a8
(0–1, 59) Ardijansjah–Makarichev, Amsterdam 1974.

10 ♘×d5
Not 10 ed ♘b4 11 ♗c4 ♗f5
12 ♖c1 ♖c8∓ – G.
10 ...                    ♘×d5
11 ♕×d5
Not 11 ed ♘b4 12 c4 ♗f5 etc.
11 ...                    ♕c7!
This improved upon 11 ...
♕×d5 12 ed ♘b4 13 000 ♗f5
14 c3 ♘×a2+ 15 ♔d2 ♘b4 16
d6! ♗×d6 17 ♔e1 ♘c2+ 18
♔f2± of Foltys–Plater, Trenčianske Teplice 1949.
12 ♕d2                   ♖d8
13 ♗d3                   ♘b4
14 00                    ♗e6
15 ♘c1 ♖ac8 16 ♖f2 ♕d7! 17
♕e2 ♕a4 18 a3 ♘×c2 19 ♗×c2
♖×c2 20 ♕×c2 ♖d1+ 21
♕×d1 ♕×d1+ 22 ♖f1 ♕d7
23 ♖f2 ½–½ Rabar–Gligorić,
Opatija 1949.

**D**

**8 00        00(79)**

Not 8 ... a5 9 ♗e3 a4 10 ♘d2
a3 11 ba! ♗e6 12 ♘c4 ♗×c4
13 ♗×c4 00 14 ♖b1! ♖×a3
15 ♖b3 ♖×b3 16 cb± Wade–
Barden, British Ch 1954.

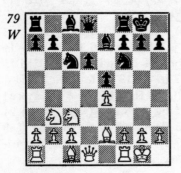

79
W

D1 9 ♗f3
D2 9 f3
D3 9 f4
D4 9 ♗e3

9 ♔h1 a5 (9 ... ♗e6 10 f4 ef
11 ♗×f4 D31) 10 a4 ♘b4 11 f4
♗e6 see D32.

**D1**

**9 ♗f3        a6**

Others:

a) **9 ... a5** 10 ♖e1!? a4 11 ♘d2
♘d4 12 ♘c1 ♗e6 13 a3 ♕b6 14
♘e3 (1–0, 54) Tarnowski–Paoli,
Debrecen 1961.

b) **9 ... ♗e6** when:

b1) **10 ♘d5** ♗×d5 11 ed ♘b8
(11 ... ♘b4 12 c4 ♖c8 13 a3 ♘a6
14 ♗e2±  – S) 12 ♗e2 ♘bd7 13
♗e3 a5 14 a4 ♖c8 15 c4 b6 16
♖a3 ♘e8 17 f4 f5= Haag–Dely,
Hungarian Ch 1964.

b2) **10 ♗e3** ♘a5 11 ♘×a5
♕×a5 12 ♕d2± – Panov and
Estrin.

c) 9 ... ♘a5 10 ♘×a5 ♕×a5
11 ♗g5! ♗e6 12 a3 takes b4
from the black queen and so
threatens 13 ♗×f6 etc. Now:

c1) **12 ... ♕c5** 13 h3 ♖fd8 14
♕d2 h6 15 ♗×f6 ♗×f6 16
♖fd1 (threatens 17 ♘d5 ♗×d5
18 ♕ × d5 with the better ending)
16 ... ♖ac8 17 ♗g4!± Botvinnik–
Kan, training game 1953.

c2) 'Rather better **12 ... ♖fd8,**
although White can still adopt
roughly the same plan as in the
game continuation' – Keres in R,
1972.

10 a4        ♘b4!?

Or 10 ... ♘a5 11 ♘×a5
♕×a5 12 ♗e3 ♗e6 13 ♕d2
♖fc8 14 ♖fd1:

a) **14 ... ♘e8** 15 h3 ♖c4 16 ♕e1
♖ac8 17 ♗d2 ♕c7 18 a5 ♗d8±
Smyslov–Holmov, 17th USSR Ch
1949.

b) **14 ... ♕b4= – G.**

11 ♗e3

After 11 ♘d5 ♘f×d5 12 ed
♗f5 it is hard for White to find
a move – Kuzminikh, 1951.

11 ...        ♗e6

12 ♕d2        ♖c8

13 ♖fd1 (13 a5!? – S) 13 ... ♕d7
14 ♖ac1 ♖fd8 with a sound
position for Black – Kuzminikh.
Evidently 9 ♗f3 is worth further
examination.

**D2**

**9 f3        a5**

Others:

a) **9 ... ♕b6+** 10 ♔h1 ♗e6 (10 ... ♖d8= – Pachman) 11 ♘d5 ♗×d5 12 ed ♘b4 13 c4 a5 14 ♗d2 a4 15 ♘c1 ♘a6 16 ♖b1 ♘c5 17 ♗c3± Bisguier–Milić, Helsinki, Olympiad 1952.

b) **9 ... ♗e6** 10 ♘d5 ♗×d5 11 ed± Geller–Barcza, Stockholm interzonal 1952.

   10 ♗e3

Or:

a) **10 ♘d5** ♘×d5 11 ed ♘b4= – B.

b) **10 a4** when:

b1) **10 ... ♗e6?** 11 ♘d5 ♘b4 12 ♘×e7+ ♕×e7 13 c3 ♘c6 14 ♗g5± Korolkov–Kuzminikh, ½-final Leningrad Ch 1948.

b2) **10 ... ♘b4!** and if 11 ♗g5 ♗e6 12 ♗×f6 ♗×f6 13 ♘d5 ♗×d5 14 ed ♗g5 15 c3 ♕b6+ 16 ♔h1 ♘a6 with a position characteristic of many open Sicilians: Black blocks the Q-side and retains quite good chances in the centre and on the K-side – Kuzminikh.

   10 ...   a4
   11 ♘c1  ♕a5

Not 11 ... a3 12 b3 ♘b4 13 ♘d3± – Pachman.

   12 ♕d2  ♘d4

Or 12 ... a3!? – S.

   13 ♗d3

According to B and S, 13 ♗×d4 ed 14 ♕×d4 d5! is bad for White, although P suggests then 15 ♗d3! de 16 ♘×e4 ♖d8 with an unclear position.

   13 ...   ♗e6
   14 a3   ♗d8

Or 14 ... d5= – G.

   15 ♔h1  ♗b6
   16 ♗g5  ♗d8
   17 ♗e3=

Pachman – Bronstein, Helsinki Olympiad 1952.

**D3**

   **9 f4**(*80*)

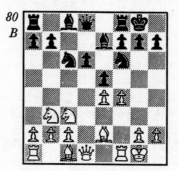

*80*
*B*

D31 9 ... ef
D32 9 ... a5!

 9 ... ♗e6 10 ♗f3 h6? 11 f5!±.

**D31**

   **9 ...**   **ef**
   10 ♗×f4  ♘e5

Others:

a) **10 ... ♕b6+!?** 11 ♔h1 ♗e6 when:

a1) **12 ♗f3** ♖ad8 13 ♕e1 ♘e5 14 ♗e2 ♘g6 15 ♗g3 d5∓ Janošević – Gligorić, Yugoslav Ch 1948.

a2) **12 ♘d5** ♗×d5 13 ed ♘e5 (13 ... ♘b4? 14 c4) 14 c4 ♘e4! 15 ♕d4 ♕×d4 16 ♘×d4 ♗f6= Sokolsky–Bronstein, ½-final 16th USSR Ch 1948.

a3) **12 ♕d2 ♘e5** (13 ♗e3 ♕c6)=
– Kuzminikh.

b) **10 ... ♗e6** when:

b1) **11 ♔h1 d5?** 12 e5 ♘e4 13
♗d3 f5 14 ef ♘×f6 15 ♕e1 ♕d7
16 ♘a4 ♗f7 17 ♘ac5± Bron-
stein–Levenfish, 17th USSR Ch
1949.

b2) **11 ♕d2 d5** (11 ... ♖c8 12
♖ad1 ♘e5 13 ♘d4 ♗d7= –
Kuzminikh) 12 e5 ♘e4 13 ♕e3
♕b6 (13 ... ♘×c3! – Kuz-
minikh) 14 ♕×b6 ab 15 ♘b5
♗g5 16 g3 ♗h3 17 ♖f3±
Aronin–Guldin, USSR Trade
Union Team Ch 1949.

b3) **11 ♗d3 ♘e5** 12 ♔h1 ♕b6 13
♕e2! ♘×d3? 14 cd ♗×b3 15
♗e3:

b31) **15 ...  ♕b4** 16 ab ♕×b3
17 ♖a5!± Botvinnik–Boleslavsky,
Sverdlovsk 1943.

b32) **15 ...  ♕c6** 16 ab d5 17
♗d4± and Black has K-side
defensive problems, as a result of
his injudicious exchanges of well-
posted pieces – Botvinnik.

11 ♘d4

Or 11 ♕d4 ♕c7 12 ♖ad1 a6
13 ♘c1 ♗e6 14 ♘g3 ♘g6 15
♗g3 ♖ac8 16 ♔h1 ♖fd8= –
Kuzminikh, 1951.

11 ...         ♗d7
12 ♔h1       ♔h8
13 ♗g3       ♗c6=

Arulaid – Bivshev, ½-final 17th
USSR Ch 1949; possibly 13 ♗e3
intending ♘f5 (G) would be
stronger, but White must be
careful of his e-pawn.

**D32**

9 ...          **a5!**
10 a4 (*81*)

Or:

a) **10 ♔h1?** a4 11 ♘d2 ef 12
♘c4 ♘×e4 13 ♘×e4 d5 14
♗×f4 de∓ Aronin–Klaman,
USSR 1957.

b) **10 ♗e3 a4:**

b1) **11 ♘c1 a3!** 12 ♘b3 (12 b3
♕a5!) 12 ... ab 13 ♖b1 ef 14
♗×f4 ♘d7 15 ♖×b2 ♗f6∓
Balogh – Pachman, Bucharest
1949.

b2) **11 ♘d2** when:

b21) **11 ... a3** 12 b3 ♘d4! 13
♘c4 b5 14 ♗×d4 (better 14 fe –
B) 14 ... ed 15 ♘×b5 ♘×e4 16
♗f3 d5 17 ♗×e4 de 18 ♕×d4
♗a6! 19 ♕×d8 ♖f×d8 20 ♘c7
♗×c4 21 bc ♖a4∓∓ Liuboshits–
Boleslavsky,  Bielorussian  Ch
1955.

b22) **11 ... ef** 12 ♖×f4 ♘e5 (or
12 ... a3!?) 13 ♘c4 ♘×c4 14
♗×c4 ♗e6 (14 ... ♘d7 15
♘d5!±) 15 ♗×e6 fe 16 a3 ♕a5
17 ♕e2 ♕a6 18 ♕×a6 ♖×a6
19 e5 de 20 ♖×a4 ♘d5=

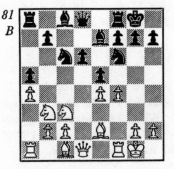

81
B

Ragozin – Rejfíř, Mariánské Lázné 1956.

10 ... ♘b4
11 ♔h1
Others:
a) 11 ♗e3 ♗e6 12 ♘d2 (12 f5 ♗×b3 13 cb d5∓ – B) 12 ... ef 13 ♖×f4 d5 14 e5 ♘d7 15 ♘f3 ♕b8∓ Grünfeld – Boleslavsky, Warsaw 1947.
b) 11 ♗f3 ♗e6 (11 ... ♕c7 12 ♗e3 ♗e6 13 ♖f2= – Bondarevsky) when:
b1) 12 f5? ♗c4 13 ♖e1? (13 ♖f2 – R, 1950) 13 ... ♘×c2! 14 ♕×c2 ♕b6+ winning a pawn; Cortlever – Kottnauer, Holland v. Czechoslovakia 1949.
b2) 12 ♔h1 ♖c8 13 f5 ♗c4 14 ♖e1 ♘d7 15 ♘d2 ♗a6 16 ♘f1 ♗×f1! 17 ♖×f1 ♘b6 18 ♕e2 ♗g5∓ Guldin – Boleslavsky, USSR Trade Union Team Ch 1949.

11 ... ♗e6
Or 11 ... ef!? 12 ♗×f4 ♗e6 – *Shakhmaty v SSSR*, 1953.

12 f5 ♗d7
Not 12 ... ♗×b3 13 cb d5 14 ed ♘×d5 15 ♗f3!± – Pachman.

13 ♗g5
Or 13 ♗b5 ♗c6 14 ♕e2 ♕c7 15 ♗g5! d5 (15 ... ♖ac8!? intending ... b5, or ... ♕c6–c4) 16 ed ♗×d5 17 ♘×d5 ♘b×d5 18 ♖ae1! h6 19 ♗h4 ♗d6 20 c4 ♘f4 21 ♕d1 ♗b4? (21 ... ♗e7 was playable.) 22 ♗×f6! ♗×e1 23 ♕g4! g5 24 ♖fe1 ♘d3 25 ♖ef1 ♕b6 26 ♗×g5! hg 27

♕×g5+ ♔h7 28 f6! 1–0 Poulsen – Stumpers, Beverwijk 1951.

13 ... ♖c8
Others:
a) 13 ... ♘×e4?? 14 ♗×e7 ♘×c3 15 bc
b) 13 ... ♗c6 14 ♗f3 (Pavlov–Suetin, Vilnius 1953) 14 ... ♘d7! – Boleslavsky, *Shakhmatny Bulletin* 1974.
c) 13 ... ♕c7!? 14 ♗f3 ♖fd8 15 ♕e2 ♖ac8 16 ♖ac1 d5 17 ed ♗f5 (Lerner–Gulko, Daugavpils 1974) 18 d6!± – Boleslavsky, 1974.

14 ♗f3 ♗c6
15 ♕e2 h6
Or 15 ... ♕c7 – R, 1950. Probably the whole line is good for Black, the note to White's 15th notwithstanding.
After the text move, Lokvenc–Gligorić, Austria v. Yugoslavia, Agram 1949, continued 16 ♗h4 (16 ♗×f6!? and 17 ♘d5 – R) 16 ... ♕c7 17 ♖ad1 ♖fd8 18 g4? (18 ♖d2) 18 ... d5!∓.

**D4**
9 ♗e3 *(82)*
White aims to put pressure on the Q-side and to concentrate his pieces against the Q-side. Pilnik was one of the main advocates of this set-up.
D41 9 ... ♗e6
D42 9 ... a5!?
**D41**
9 ... ♗e6
10 ♗f3

82
B

Also:

a) **10 f4** when:

a1) **10 ... a5?!** (Sterner–Boleslavsky, Sweden v. USSR 1954) 11 f5! (11 fe was played.) 11 ... ♗c8 12 ♗c4 a4 13 ♘d2 a3 14 b3 ♘b4 15 ♘d5 ♘b×d5 16 ♗×d5 ♘×d5 17 ed± – B.

a2) **10 ... d5** (10 ... ef!?) 11 f5 (11 fe ♘×e5= or 11 ed ♘×d5 12 ♘×d5 ♗×d5= – S) 11 ... d4! 12 fe fe 13 ♗c4 dc 14 ♗×e6+ ♔h8 15 bc ♕×d1 16 ♖a×d1 ♘×e4= Idelchik–Barsky, Vilnius 1953.

b) **10 ♕d2** a5 and now:

b1) **11 a4** ♘b4 12 ♖fd1 (12 f4 ♖c8) 12 ... ♕c7? (12 ... d5 13 ed ♘f×d5 14 ♘×d5 ♘×d5= – Kuzminikh) 13 ♖ac1 ♖ac8 14 f3 d5 15 ♘b5 ♕b8 16 ed ♘f×d5 17 ♗a7 ♕a8 18 c4 ♘f4 Yudovich – Konstantinopolosky, Moscow Ch 1949; Black has K-side chances, but is in danger on the Q-side.

b2) **11 ♖ad1** a4 12 ♘c1 ♕a5 13 f3 ♖fc8 14 a3 ♘d4 15 ♗×d4 ed 16 ♘b5 d5∓ Drozd–Partos, Romania 1966.

After 10 ♗f3:
D411 10 ... ♘a5
D412 10 ... a5

10 ... ♗c4? 11 ♖e1 ♖c8 12 ♖c1 a5 13 ♘d5 ♘×d5 14 ed ♘b4 15 a3 ♘a6 16 ♘d2 ♗b5 17 c4± S. Nedeljković–Janošević, Split 1949.

**D411**

**10 ...** ♘a5

11 ♘×a5 ♕×a5

12 ♕d2

Or 12 ♖e1!?, preparing ♘d5.

12 ... ♖fc8!

13 ♖fd1

Not 13 ♘d5? ♕×d2 14 ♘×e7+ ♔f8 15 ♗×d2 ♖×c2! 16 ♗c3 ♔×e7 17 ♗d1 ♖×c3! 18 bc ♘×e4∓ – G.

13 ... ♕b4

14 ♖ab1

Or 14 ♘d5 ♘×d5 15 ed ♕×d2 16 ♖×d2 (Janošević–Joppen, Belgrade 1954) 16 ... ♗f5 – R.

14 ... h6

Or 14 ... a6 15 a3 (15 ♗g5!?) 15 ... ♕c4 16 ♗g5 ♖d8 17 b3 ♕c7 18 a4:

a) **18 ...** ♘e8 19 ♗×e7 ♕×e7 20 a5± Pilnik–Taimanov, Saltsjöbaden interzonal 1952.

b) **18 ...** ♖ac8 19 ♗×f6 ♗×f6 20 ♘d5 ♕×c2 (20 ... ♗×d5 21 ♕×d5±) 21 ♘×f6+ gf 22 ♕h6! (± S) 22 ... ♕c7 23 ♕×f6 ♖d7! with a tenable game for Black; Unzicker–Pachman, Saltsjöbaden interzonal 1952.

15 a3 ♕c4

16 ♗e2    ♕c7

Pilnik – Janošević, Belgrade 1954, went instead 16 ... ♕c6 17 f3 a6 18 ♖bc1 ♗c4 (18 ... b5!?; 18 ... ♘d7!?) 19 b3 ♗×e2 20 ♘×e2 b5 21 ♘g3 ♗f8 22 ♘f5± (1–0, 31).

   17 f3       a6
   18 ♖bc1   ♘d7
   19 ♗f1    b5±

20 a4 b4 21 ♘d5 ♗×d5 22 ♕×d5 ♘c5 23 b3 (23 c3! – Winter) 23 ... ♗g5! This exchanging manoeuvre should probably not have been permitted. Now after 24 ♗×g5 hg:

a) **25 ♔h1** ($\frac{1}{2}-\frac{1}{2}$, 41) Boleslavsky–Euwe, Zürich candidates' 1953

b) **25 ♕×d6** ♕×d6 26 ♖×d6 ♘×b3 27 ♖b1± Unzicker–Kupper, Chaumont 1958.

**D412**

   **10 ...**     **a5**(*83*)

83
W

   11 ♘d5

Or 11 ♕d2 (11 a4? ♘b4) 11 ... a4 12 ♘c1 a3 13 b3 ♕a5 14 ♖d1= S. Nedeljković–Marković, Belgrade 1949.

   11 ...     ♗×d5

11 ... a4!? is interesting, e.g. 12 ♗b6? (better 12 ♘d2) 12 ... ♕c8! 13 ♘d2 ♗×d5 14 ed ♘b4 15 c4 ♘d7 16 ♗e3 f5 17 g3 f4 18 gf ef 19 ♗d4 ♗f6∓ Lehmann–Stein, W. Germany v. Ukraine 1970.

   12 ed     ♘b8!

Or 12 ... ♘b4 when:

a) **13 c3** ♘a6 14 a4 ♘d7 15 ♗e2 f5 Pilnik–S. Nedeljković, Belgrade 1952.

b) **13 a3** ♘a6 14 c4 (14 ♕d2! a4 15 ♘a5! – R, 1952) 14 ... ♘d7 15 ♗e2 a4 16 ♘d2 f5 17 f4 ♘ac5= S. Nedeljković–Marić, Split 1949.

The text move has the subtle idea of luring White's pawns on to white squares, after which an exchange of dark-squared bishops will give Black chances on the weakened dark squares.

   13 c4!?

Others:

a) **13 a4?** ♘bd7 14 ♗e2 ♘b6! 15 c4 ♘bd7! 16 ♘d2 ♘e8 17 ♔h1 ♗g5! 18 ♗×g5 ♕×g5 19 ♖a3 ♕e7∓ Pilnik – Petrosian, Buenos Aires 1954.

b) **13 ♕d3** when:

b1) **13 ... ♘fd7** 14 ♗g4! ♕c7 15 a4 ♘b6 16 ♘d2 ♘8d7 (Pilnik – Smyslov, Amsterdam candidates' 1956) 17 c3 intending 18 ♕b5± – S.

b2) **13 ... ♕c7** 14 a4 ♘bd7 15 ♕b5 ♖fc8 16 ♖fc1 g6 17 ♗e2 ♘e4 18 f3 ♘ec5 19 ♘d2 ♘b6

20 ♗c4 ½–½ Djurašević–Sofrevski,
Yugoslav Ch 1958.

13 ...                ♘a6
14 ♗d2              b6
15 ♗c3              c5∓
16 ♘×c5 bc 17 ♕e1 ♘d7 18
♗d1 a4 19 ♗c2 f5 20 ♖d1 (20
f3!?) 20 ... g6 21 ♕e2 ♗f6 22
f3 e4! 23 ♗×f6 ♕×f6 24 fe
f4! 25 ♖f2 ♘e5 26 ♖df1 ♕h4
27 ♗d1 ♖f7 28 ♕c2 g5 29 ♕c3
♖af8 30 h3 h5 31 ♗e2?! (31
♗×a4 g4 32 ♗d1 ♔h7 and
33 ... f3) 31 ... g4 32 ♖×f4?
♖×f4 33 ♖×f4 ♖×f4 34 g3
♘f3+ 35 ♔f2 ♕×h3 36 gf g3+
37 ♔×f3 g2+ 38 ♔f2 ♕h2 0–1
Pilnik–Geller, Göteborg interzonal 1955.

**D42**
9 ...                a5!?*(84)*

84
W

D421 10 ♗f3
D422 10 ♘d2
D423 10 a4
a) **10 ♔h1** a4 11 ♘d2 a3 12 ♘c4
ab 13 ♖b1 ♗e6 14 ♖×b2 d5
(∓ S) 15 ed ♘×d5 16 ♘×d5
♗×d5 17 ♗b6 (17 ♘b6 ♖×a2)

17 ... ♕d7 18 ♗f3 (Alexander–
Janošević, Belgrade 1952) 18 ...
♗e6= – G.
b) **10 a3** ♗e6 (or 10 ... a4 11
♘d2 ♘d4!∓) 11 ♗f3 a4 12 ♘c1
♕a5 13 ♘1a2 ♘d7 14 ♘d5
♗×d5 15 ed ♘d4! 16 ♗×d4 ed
17 ♕×d4 ♗f6 18 ♕g4 ♘e5 19
♕e4 ♘×f3+ 20 ♕×f3 ♕d2!∓
S. Nikolić–Gligorić, Yugoslav Ch
1965.
c) **10 f3** a4 11 ♘c1 a3 12 ♖b1
♗e6 (12 ... ab= – S) 13 ♘d5
♗×d5 14 ed ♘b4 15 c4 ♘d7!
16 ba ♖×a3 17 ♕d2 (17 ♖b4?
♖×e3) 17 ... ♘a6 18 ♖×b7
♘ac5 19 ♖b2 ♕c7 20 ♘b3
♖fa8 21 ♖fb1 ♕a7!∓ and not
22 ♖c2? ♗g5! 23 ♔f2 f5∓∓
Janošević–Matulović,   Belgrade
1955.

**D421**
10 ♗f3              a4
11 ♘d2
Or 11 ♘c1 ♕a5 (11 ... a3 12
b3 ♕a5∓ – S) 12 a3 ♗e6 13
♘d5 ♗×d5 14 ed ♘b8 15 c4
♘bd7= Znosko–Borovski v.
Maller, Lugano 1949.
11 ...                a3
11 ... ♗e6!? 12 ♘d5 ♗×d5
13 ed ♘d4!? is less consistent.
12 b3!
Not 12 ba ♕a5! 13 ♘d5
♘×d5 14 ed ♘d4 15 ♗×d4 ed
16 ♘b3 ♕×a3∓ Matanović–
Gligorić, Saltsjöbaden interzonal
1952.
12 ...                ♘b4
13 ♘c4              ♗e6

14 ♘b6    ♖a6

a) **15 ♘ca4?!** d5!∓ Karaklajić–Gligorić, Opatija 1949.

b) **15 ♘bd5!** (Gligorić) 15 ... ♘b×d5 16 ♘×d5 ♘×d5 17 ed ♗d7 18 ♗e2 ♖a8 19 c4 f5 20 f3 ♗g5 21 ♗f2 e4?! 22 ♗d4 ef 23 ♗×f3 ♕c7 24 ♕c2 ♗f6 25 ♕d3 b5 26 ♖ac1 bc 27 bc ♗×d4+ 28 ♕×d4 (1–0, 44) Yankov–Holm, Primorsko 1974.

**D422**

    **10 ♘d2**    d5!?

Others:

a) **10 ... ♘d4** when:

a1 **11 ♘c4** b5! 12 ♗×d4 bc 13 ♗e3 ♗e6= – G.

a2) **11 ♗×d4** ed 12 ♘b5 ♕b6 13 a4!± – Paoli, *Informator* 10.

b) **10 ... ♗e6** 11 ♘c4 b5!? (Janošević– Fuderer, Belgrade 1952) 12 ♘×b5! ♘×e4 13 f3 d5 14 fe! (14 ♘b6 ♖b8 15 fe d4!) 14 ... dc 15 ♕×d8 ♖a×d8 16 c3± – G.

    11 ed       ♘×d5
    12 ♘×d5    ♕×d5
    13 ♘c4     ♕×d1
    14 ♖f×d1   ♗e6

Or 14 ... ♗f5 (14 ... ♘b4 15 ♘b6!) 15 c3 ♖fd8 (Pilnik–Schweber, Mar del Plata 1966) 16 ♗b6!±.

    15 c3       f5

After 15 ... ♖fd8 16 ♗b6 ♖×d1+ 17 ♖×d1 ♗d8 18 ♗e3 ♗e7 19 a4 it is harder to hold the ending; Unzicker–Matanović, Opatija 1953.

    16 ♘d6    ♘d4!

Not 16 ... ♖fd8 17 ♘×b7 ♖×d1+ 18 ♖×d1 ♖b8 19 ♗a6!

    17 ♗×d4    ♗×d6
    18 ♗b6±

Paoli–Liptay, Debrecen 1970; S gives this as =.

**D423**

    **10 a4**(*85*)

85
B

D4231 10 ... ♗e6
D4232 10 ... ♘b4!

**D4231**

    **10 ...**       ♗e6
    11 f4

Or:

a) **11 ♔h1?!** ♘b4! 12 f4 ♕c7 13 ♗f3 ♖fd8 14 ♖f2 d5!∓ Radev–Spassov, Varna 1973.

b) **11 ♗f3** ♘b4 12 ♕e2 ♕c8 13 ♖fc1 ♗c4 14 ♕d1 ♕e6 15 ♘d2 ♗a6= S. Nedeljković–Milić, Yugoslav Ch 1951.

    11 ...       d5!

Not 11 ... ef 12 ♖×f4 ♘d7?! 13 ♘d4!±.

    12 f5       d4
    13 fe       dc

13 ... fe may be better.

14 ef+

Ghizdavu gave 14 ♗c4 fe 15 ♗×e6+ ♚h8 16 bc ♕×d1 17 ♖a×d1 ♘×e4= in *The Chess Player*. The bishop looks better left at e2.

14 ...          ♚h8
15 bc           ♕×d1
16 ♖a×d1   ♘×e4

The position is complicated, but perhaps not bad for Black – AHM.

**D4232**

10 ...          ♘b4!
11 f4

Others:

a) 11 ♗f3 ♗e6 12 ♕e2 ♕c8 13 ♖fc1 ♗c4 14 ♕d1 ♕e6∓ S. Nedeljković–Milić, Yugoslav Ch 1951.

b) 11 ♚h1 d5 12 ed ♘f×d5 13 ♘×d5 ♘×d5 14 ♗d2 (14 ♗c5!?) 14 ... ♗e6 15 ♗f3

♕c7∓ (0–1, 27) Buzhlinkham–Kozlovskaya, Lipetsk 1974.

11 ...          ♗e6
12 f5?!        ♗×b3
13 cb           d5

14 ed ♘f×d5 15 ♘×d5 ♘×d5 16 ♗f2 e4 17 ♗c4 e3 18 ♗e1 ♘f6 19 ♕e2 ♗c5 20 ♗c3 ♕b6 21 ♚h1 ♖ad8 22 ♕f3 ♖fe8∓ (0–1, 37) Bibilashvili–Ubilava, Georgian Ch 1974.

## Conclusion

Although the most popular move, 7 ♘b3 gives Black good counterplay based on an early ... a5 in most variations. The trickiest lines are those where White strives for piece control of d5, by 7 ... ♗e7 8 ♗e3 OO 9 ♕d2 (p. 89) or 8 OO OO 9 ♗f3 (D1), but if Black can keep the position fluid he should be all right.

# 10 Sixth Move Rarities

The first question that Black should ask himself, if after 1 e4 c5 2 ♘f3 ♘c6 3 d4 cd 4 ♘×d4 ♘f6 5 ♘c3 d6(*86*) White plays some move other than 6 ♗e2, is 'Can I play ... e5 just the same?'. For when ... e5 can be played without disadvantage, it is usually the speediest and most active way of getting counter-chances. In a few cases, however, we shall see that Black must renounce ... e5 in favour of some other means.

*86*
W

The main alternatives:
A 6 f4
B 6 g3
C 6 ♗e3

plus two moves which have already been extensively treated

in earlier volumes in the Batsford series:

a) **6 ♗c4** (Sozin) against which 6 ... e5!? has been tried, although 7 ♘f5 and 7 ♘de2 ought to give White a slight positional advantage (op. cit. p. 174–6).

b) **6 ♗g5** (Richter–Rauzer) when 6 ... e5?! is definitely suspect in view of 7 ♗×f6 gf (7 ... ♕×f6 8 ♘d5 ♕d8 9 ♘b5) 8 ♘f5 – G.

plus a variety of rare and more or less ineffectual moves:

a) **6 ♗b5** was one of the earliest moves ever to be tried from diagram *86*. Evidently 6 ... e5? is a blunder in this case, but Black can turn the game into a Dragon variation, e.g. 6 ... ♗d7 7 00 g6! 8 h3 ♗g7 9 ♗e3 00 10 ♘de2 when:

a1) Mackenzie – L. Paulsen, Frankfurt 1887, continued **10 ... a6?** 11 ♗d3 ♘e5 12 f4±.

a2) Black could equalize, for example, by **10 ... ♘a5** 11 ♗d3 ♕c8 controlling the thematic c4 square.

b) **6 f3** weakens the black squares:
b1) **6 ... e5!?** 7 ♘b3 h6 8 ♗c4

♗e7 9 ♗e3 00 10 ♕d2 ♗e6 11 ♗d5 ♗×d5 12 ♘×d5 ♘×d5 13 ♕×d5 a5∓ Matanović–Kostić, Vinkovci 1948.

b2) **6 ... ♕b6!?** e.g. 7 ♗e3!? ♕×b2 8 ♘db5 ♕b4! 9 ♘c7+ ♔d8 10 ♘×a8 ♕×c3+ 11 ♔f2 ♗e6 with an unclear position – AHM.

b3) **6 ... e6** (intending ... d5 – S), 6 ... ♗d7 and 6 ... g6 are also playable.

c) **6 h3** is a waiting move, preparing g4 in some cases. In practice Black has been suspicious of lines like 6 ... e5 7 ♘f3 h6 8 ♗c4, and instead prefers (following S):

c1) **6 ... a6** 7 g4 ♘×d4 (7 ... e5 8 ♘de2 ♗e7 9 ♗e3 00 10 ♘g3±) 8 ♕×d4 e5 9 ♕d3 ♗e6 10 ♗g2 ♗e7:

c11) **11 b3?** 00 12 ♗b2 b5 13 000? b4 14 ♘e2 a5 15 f4 ♘d7 16 f5 ♘c5∓ Gereben–Geller, Budapest 1952.

c12) **11 f4** ♖c8 12 f5 ♗c4 13 ♕f3 d5!? 14 ed e4 15 ♘×e4 ♘×e4 16 ♕×e4 00 with compensation for the pawns.

c2) **6 ... e6** 7 g4 is a timid form of the Keres Attack against the Scheveningen variation Black can play:

c21) **7 ... a6** 8 ♗g2 ♕c7 9 00 ♗e7=.

c22) **7 ... d5!?** 8 ♗g2 ♗b4 9 ed ♘×d5 10 00=.

c3) **6 ... g6** is of course also good.

d) **6 ♘b3** avoids ... e5 by putting immediate pressure on the d-file and holding back the development of the king's bishop. Black's best reply is 6 ... a6! 7 a4 g6! 8 ♗e2 ♗g7 9 00 00 10 f4 ♗e6:

d1) **11 ♗e3** ♘a5 12 f5 ♗c4 13 ♗d3 = – S.

d2) **11 ♗f3** ♘a5 12 ♘×a5 ♕×a5 13 ♘d5 ♘×d5 14 ed ♗d7 15 ♖e1 ♖fe8 16 c3 b5∓ Westerinen–Suetin, Sochi 1974.

e) **6 ♘de2** has a similar basis; 6 ... e5 would be dubious after 7 ♘g3. So:

e1) **6 ... e6** 7 g3 d5! (7 ... ♗e7 Kagan–Geller, Petropolis 1973) 8 ed ♘×d5:

e11) **9 ♗g2** ♘×c3 10 ♕×d8+ ♘×d8 11 ♘×c3 ♗d7 12 ♗e3 ♗b4 13 ♗d4 ♗c6!= Euwe–Pirc, match 1949.

e12) **9 ♘×d5** ed 10 ♗g2 ♗f5! and White cannot play 11 ♗×d5 because of 11 ... ♘b4! 12 ♗b3 ♕×d1+ 13 ♔×d1 000+ 14 ♗d2 ♗c5∓ – P.

e2) **6 ... a6** 7 ♘f4? (7 g3!?) 7 ... e6= Aitken–Matanović, Bad Pyrmont 1951.

**A**

**6 f4** e5!? (*87*)

Others:

a) **6 ... g6** Dragon Variation, Levenfish Attack.

b) **6 ... e6** 7 ♗e3 ♗e7 8 ♗e2 00 9 00 e5!? (9 ... ♗d7 Scheveningen Variation) see Karpov–Spassky, p. xv.

c) **6 ... ♗g4** 7 ♕d3 g6 8 ♘×c6 (8 ♗e3!? – S) 8 ... bc 9 h3 ♗e6 10 ♗e2 ♗g7 11 00 ♕b6 12 ♔h1

♘d7 13 ♖b1 a5 14 ♗e3 ♕c7 15 ♗d4± Parma–Ničevski, Yugoslav Ch 1975.

d) 6 ... ♕b6 7 ♘b3 e6 8 ♗d3 d5 9 e5 ♘d7 10 ♕e2 ♘c5! when:

d1) 11 ♗b5! a6 12 ♗×c6= ♕×c6= Parma–Dueball, Dortmund 1973.

d2) 11 ♗e3? d4! 12 ♗×d4 (12 ♘×d4? ♕×b2 13 ♔d2 ♘a4!) 12 ... ♘×d4 13 ♘×d4 ♕×b2∓ – Dueball in *The Chess Player*.

87
W

7 ♘f3

Or 7 ♘×c6 bc 8 fe:

a) 8 ... de 9 ♕×d8+ ♔×d8 10 ♗c4±.

b) 8 ... ♘g4!? 9 ed ♗×d5 with compensation – S.

  7 ...          ♗e7
  8 ♗c4          00

Not 8 ... ♗e6 9 ♗×e6 fe 10 f5! ef 11 ef d5 12 ♗g5 d4 13 ♗×f6 ♗×f6 14 ♘e4± – Marić, *Informator 2*.

  9 f5!?          ♕b6
  10 ♗b3          h6
  11 g4!?

a) 11 ... ♘×g4? 12 ♕e2 ♘d4

13 ♘×d4 ♗h4+ 14 ♔f1 ♕×d4 15 ♖g1!:

a1) 15 ... ♕f2+ 16 ♕×f2 ♘×f2 17 ♗×h6 ♔h7 18 ♗g5! 1–0 Bronstein–Barczay, Szombathely 1966.

a2) 15 ... h5 16 ♖×g4! hg 17 ♗e3 ♕b4 18 ♕g4 ♗d8 19 ♗×h6 ♗f6 20 ♘d5±±

b) Maric suggested 11 ... d5! e.g.:

b1) 12 ed e4 13 dc ef 14 ♕×f3 ♗b4=.

b2) 12 ♗×d5 ♗b4 13 g5 ♘×d5 14 gf e4 with complications;

b3) 12 ♘×d5 ♘×d5 13 ♗×d5 ♘d4! 14 ♘×d4 ♗h4+ 15 ♔f1 ed is also unclear.

**B**

  **6 g3**(*88*)

The idea here too was to make ... e5 unattractive. White thinks he can control d5 more effectively with his bishop bearing down from the flank.

88
B

B1 6 ... e5!?
B2 6 ... ♗g4

a) 6 ... ♕b6 7 ♘b3 e6 8 ♗e3 ♕c7 9 f4 a6 10 a4 b6 11 ♗g2

♖b8 12 00 ♗e7 13 g4±
Enevoldsen–Barcza, Berlin 1962.

b) **6 ...** ♘×**d4** 7 ♕×d4 g6 8
♗g2 ♗g7 Dragon.

c) **6 ... g6** 7 ♘4e2 (7 ♗g2 ♗g7
Dragon) 7 ... h5!? 8 h3 ♗d7 9
♗g2 ♕c8 – Tal.

d) **6 ... e6** and 6 ... a6 also come
into consideration.

**B1**

**6 ...                    e5!?**

Black goes ahead willy-nilly.

7 ♘de2          ♗e7

Others:

a) **7 ... d5!?** 8 ed ♘b4 9 a3
♘b×d5 10 ♗g2 ♗e6 11 ♗g5
♗c5 12 00 ♘×c3 13 ♘×c3
00!? 14 ♗×b7 ♖b8 15 ♕f3 ♗e7
16 ♗×f6 ♗×f6 17 ♖ab1 ♕b6
18 ♗e4 (1–0, 41) Kagan–Tan,
Petropolis interzonal 1973.

b) **7 ...** ♗**g4** 8 ♗g2:

b1) **8 ...** ♗**e7** 9 h3 ♗e6 10 b3
00 11 ♗b2 ♕a5 12 00 ♖fd8 13
♘d5 (1–0, 41) Kieninger–van
Seters, Beverwijk 1951.

b2) **8 ...** ♘**d4** 9 00 ♖c8 (9 ...
♘f3+? 10 ♔h1 h5 11 ♕d3) 10
h3 ♗×e2!? (10 ... ♘×e2+
11 ♘×e2 ♗e6±) 11 ♘×e2
♘×c2 12 ♖b1 ♗e7 (12 ... ♘b4
13 ♕b3) 13 ♗d2 00 14 ♗c3 b5
15 ♖c1 (Boleslavsky–Shagalovich,
Bielorussian Ch 1955) 15 ... b4
16 ♗d2 ♕c7 17 ♗×b4 ♕b6!
18 ♗c3 ♘b4 19 ♖a1 ♖c7 with
counter-chances for Black – G.

8 ♗g2          00

Or 8 ... h6 9 h3 ♖b8 10 00 b5
11 ♗e3 ♕d7 12 a3 ♗d8?! 13

♕d2 00 14 ♖fd1 ♗c7 15 g4±
Milić–Puc, Yugoslav Ch 1951.

9 00          a6

Or 9 ... ♗e6 (R, 1956) 10
♘d5± – S.

10 h3          b5
11 ♗e3          b4

Or 11 ... ♘a5 12 b3 ♕c7 13
♕d2 ♗b7 14 g4 ♖ac8 15 ♖ac1
♖fd8 16 ♘d5± Keller–Gromek,
Moscow 1956.

12 ♘d5          ♘×d5
13 ed          ♘a5
14 b3          ♘b7

15 ♕d2 a5 16 a3 ba 17 ♖×a3±
Boleslavsky–Bondarevsky, USSR
1953.

**B2**

**6 ...                    ♗g4** (*89*)

89
W

7 f3

7 ♕d3 can be met by:

a) **7 ...** ♘×**d4** 8 ♕×d4 ♗f3 9
♗b5+ ♘d7 10 00± – R, 1956.

b) **7 ...** ♗**d7** 8 ♗g2 g6 9 00 ♗g7
10 ♘b3 ♖c8! 'when it turns out
that White's queen is worse off on
d3 than on d1' – G.

7 ...          ♗d7

Not 7 ... ♘×d4 8 ♕×d4

♗×f3? (safer 8 ... ♗d7±) 9
♗b5+ ♘d7 10 ♖f1! 'even better
than 10 00) 10 ... ♗g4 11 ♕d5!
♗e6 (11 ... e6 12 ♕×b7) 12
♕×b7 g6 13 ♘d5! ♖c8
(Augustin–Smejkal, Czech Ch
1966) 14 c3 ♗g7 15 ♗e3 00 16
♗×a7 going for a winning ending
– Kottnauer, *Schakend Nederland*.

8 ♗g2
8 ♗e3 is more active:
a) **8 ... e6** 9 ♕d2 a6 with a form
of Najdorf Variation, e.g. 10 000
♕c7 or 10 g4 ♗e7= – AHM;
b) **8 ... g6** 9 ♕d2 ♗g7 10 000 00
11 g4 is a passive Dragon:
c) **8 ... ♘×d4** 9 ♕×d4 ♗c6 10
♕d2 e6 11 000± Trifunović–
Pomar, Palma 1966.
d) **8 ... e5** 9 ♘de2 ♗e6
Grigoriev–Stolyar, USSR 1953.

8 ...          a6
Or 8 ... g6 9 ♘ce2 ♘×d4 10
♘×d4 ♗g7 11 c3 00=
Kieninger–Rellstab, Bad Elster
1938.

9 ♘b3
Fuderer–Najdorf, Bled 1950,
went 9 ♗e3 e6 10 00 ♗e7 11 ♕e2
♕c7 12 ♖ad1 b5 13 ♕d2 00 14
h3 b4 15 ♘ce2 d5 with counterplay.

9 ...          e6
10 ♗e3          b5
Or 10 ... ♗e7 11 ♘a4 00 12
♘b6 ♖b8 13 ♘×d7 ♕×d7 14
00 ♕c7 15 ♕e2 d5= Aitken–
Gligorić, Bad Pyrmont 1951.

11 f4          ♖c8
12 00          ♗e7

13 ♔h1          ♕c7
14 a3          00=
Pfeiffer–Ivkov, W. Germany v.
Yugoslavia 1960.

**C**

6 ♗e3 (90)
This is sometimes played to
reach the Sozin Attack while
avoiding the line 6 ♗c4 ♕b6. A
full treatment of the 6 ♗e3
variants was given in chapter 18
of *The Sicilian Sozin*. This section
is a summary (and in a few cases
an updating) of that chapter.

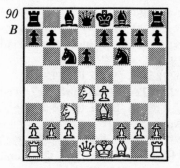

90
B

6 ...          e5!?
Consistent with the theme of
this book, 6 ... e5 will at least
appeal to lovers of the Lasker
Variation. Apart from 6 ... e6
or 6 ... ♗d7, Black can also
strike out on an original tack
with 6 ... ♘g4!?:
a) **7 ♗g5!?** (Velimirović) 7 ...
♕b6 8 ♗b5 ♗d7 9 00 ♕×d4 10
♗×c6 ♕×d1 11 ♗×d7+
♔×d7 12 ♖f×d1 h6! intending
... g5 – Botterill and Harding.
b) **7 ♗b5** ♘×e3 8 fe ♗d7 9 00

e6! (9 ... ♘e5? 10 ♘f3!±±) 10 ♗×c6 bc:

b1) **11 e5** ♗e7! 12 ♕h5 00 13 ed ♗×d6 14 ♘e4 ♗e7 15 ♖ad1 ♕c7 16 ♘b3 (Karaklajić–Taimanov, Moscow 1956) 16 ... h6= – G.

b2) **11 ♕f3**:

b21) **11 ... ♕e7** 12 e5 d5 13 b4! g6 14 b5 c5 (14 ... ♗g7 is a little better.) 15 e4! ♗g7 (15 ... cd 16 ed ♖c8 17 ♘e4! – Kapengut) 16 ed 00 17 ♘c6! ♗×c6 18 dc ♗×e5 19 ♖ae1 (19 ♖ad1!? ♕h4 20 g3 ♕c4 – Kapengut) 19 ... ♕c7 20 ♔h1! (or 20 ♘e4) Kapengut–Kupreichik, Minsk Spartakiad 1974.

b22) **11 ... ♕f6** 12 ♕e2:

b221) **12 ... ♕d8** 13 e5 ♗e7 14 ed ♗×d6 15 ♖ad1 00 16 ♘f3± – Kapengut.

b222) **12 ... ♕g5** 13 ♖f3 ♕c5 14 ♖af1 f6 15 ♖g3 ♔e7 and now 16 e5!? (Kapengut) or 16 ♕a6 (Suetin) with an obscure position in either case.

    7 ♘db5

Others:

a) **7 ♘b3** ♗e6 (Ostojić–Gufeld,

Skopje 1970) 8 ♗g5 (or 8 ♕d2) 8 ... ♗e7 9 ♕d2 h5 10 ♗×f6 ♗×f6 = – P.

b) **7 ♘de2!?** ♗e7 8 g3:

b1) **8 ... 00** 9 ♗g2 ♗d7 10 00 ♕c8 11 ♘d5!± Ghizdavu–Mititelu, Romanian Ch 1973.

b2) **8 ... ♘g4** 9 ♘d5 ♘×e3 10 fe! ♗g4 11 ♕d3! (11 ♕d2 ♗f3!∓ – Velimirović) 11 ... ♕a5 12 ♘ec3 00 13 ♗e2 ♗e6 14 000 (14 00! is critical – Ghizdavu.) 14 ... ♗×d5! 15 ♕×d5 ♕×d5! 16 ♘×d5 ½-½ Ghizdavu–Gheorghiu, Romanian Ch 1973; evidently this line needs further consideration.

After 7 ♘db5 the game transposes to the Lasker Variation (p. 48).


Conclusion

Most of these rare sixth moves are innocuous, although lines based on ... e6 or ... g6 may in some cases be better than ... e5. A positional trap to note is that it is unfavourable to meet 6 g3 by 6 ... ♗g4, and 6 ♗e3 ♘g4!? is also a line best avoided by Black.

# Index

# Index of Complete Games

Numbers in bold indicate the players with White.